PUBLIC SECTOR UNIONS
IN THE AGE OF AUSTERITY

PUBLIC SECTOR UNIONS IN THE AGE OF AUSTERITY

EDITED BY
STEPHANIE ROSS
AND LARRY SAVAGE

FERNWOOD PUBLISHING • HALIFAX & WINNIPEG

Editing: Marianne Ward
Text design: Brenda Conroy
Cover design: John van der Woude
Printed and bound in Canada

Published in Canada by Fernwood Publishing
32 Oceanvista Lane, Black Point, Nova Scotia, B0J 1B0
and 748 Broadway Avenue, Winnipeg, Manitoba, R3G 0X3
www.fernwoodpublishing.ca

Fernwood Publishing Company Limited gratefully acknowledges the financial support
of the Government of Canada through the Canada Book Fund and the Canada Council
for the Arts, the Nova Scotia Department of Communities, Culture and Heritage,
the Manitoba Department of Culture, Heritage and Tourism under the
Manitoba Publishers Marketing Assistance Program and the Province of Manitoba,
through the Book Publishing Tax Credit, for our publishing program.

Library and Archives Canada Cataloguing in Publication

Public sector unions in the age of austerity
/ edited by Stephanie Ross & Larry Savage.

(Labour in Canada; 4)
Includes bibliographical references.
ISBN 978-1-55266-584-8 (pbk.)

1. Labor unions—Political activity—Canada. I. Ross, Stephanie, 1970-,
editor of compilation II. Savage, Larry, 1977-, editor of compilation
III. Series: Labour in Canada (Halifax, N.S.); 4

HD6527.P64 2013   331.880971   C2013-903047-6

CONTENTS

LABOUR IN CANADA SERIES 7

INTRODUCTION: PUBLIC SECTOR UNIONS IN THE AGE OF AUSTERITY (Stephanie Ross and Larry Savage) 9
　Defining the Public Sector 10
　Understanding Public Sector Labour Relations 13
　Public Sector Union Responses to Neoliberal Austerity 13
　Lessons from Public Sector Union Struggles 14
　Conclusion 16

1. WHEN YOUR BOSS IS THE STATE: THE PARADOXES OF PUBLIC SECTOR WORK (Bryan Evans) 18
　Public Sector Unions in Historical Perspective 19
　Public Sector Labour Relations in a Neoliberal Era 21
　What Makes Working for the State Different? 28

2. THE CONTINUING ASSAULT ON PUBLIC SECTOR UNIONS (Leo Panitch and Donald Swartz) 31
　From Consent to Coercion 32
　Permanent Exceptionalism and the Charter 33
　Permanent Exceptionalism in the Twenty-First Century 36
　Labour Rights and the Courts 38
　The Current Crisis and Labour Rights 41
　Conclusion 44

3. PUBLIC SECTOR UNIONS AND ELECTORAL POLITICS IN CANADA (Larry Savage and Charles W. Smith) 46
　A Brief History of Public Sector Unions and Electoral Politics 47
　Testing the Waters: Public Sector Unions and Electoral Politics, 1960–1990 48
　Public Sector Unions, Social Democracy and Electoral Politics in the Neoliberal Era, 1990–20132 52
　The Future of Public Sector Unions and Electoral Politics 54

4. SOCIAL UNIONISM AND UNION POWER IN PUBLIC SECTOR UNIONS (Stephanie Ross) 57
　Defining Social Unionism 57
　Sources of Social Unionism in Public Sector Unions 59
　Public Sector Unions, Union Power and Social Unionism 64

5. RENEWING PUBLIC SECTOR UNIONS (David Camfield) 69
　Threats to Public Sector Unions 69
　Union Renewal and Union Power 72
　An Alternative: Social Movement Unionism 75
　How to Change the Unions? 77

6. UNIONS IN THE NONPROFIT SOCIAL SERVICES SECTOR: GENDERED RESISTANCE (Donna Baines) 80
　Overview of the Nonprofit Social Services 81
　Unique Aspects: Care, Altruism, Social Justice 82
　Unions in the Nonprofit Sector 84
　Restructuring and Managerialism 84
　Precarious Work 85

    Resistance and New Union Forms 86

    Conclusions 89

7. IN THE PUBLIC INTEREST: NURSES ON STRIKE (Linda Briskin) 91

    Nursing Work and Health Care Restructuring 91

    Public Sector Strikes, Feminization of Militancy and Nurses' Strikes 93

    The Public Interest and the Politicization of Caring 95

    The Public Trust 98

    Conclusion 100

8. CLASSROOM STRUGGLE: TEACHERS' UNIONS, COLLECTIVE BARGAINING
    AND NEOLIBERAL EDUCATION REFORM (Andy Hanson) 103

    The Contradictory Role of Public Education: State-Capitalism Linkages 104

    Legislating Education: From the Public Education Project to Collective Bargaining 105

    Who Negotiates: Provincial and Local Negotiations 107

    Legislation to Reverse Teachers' Gains: Reform and Retrenchment 108

    Union Activism: Making Gains in Neoliberal Times 110

    Conclusion 112

9. THE PARADOX OF PROFESSIONALISM: UNIONS OF PROFESSIONALS IN THE PUBLIC SECTOR
    (Larry Savage and Michelle Webber) 114

    Professionals and Unions 115

    Professionalism, Deprofessionalization and Professional Work 116

    Strategies and Institutional Characteristics of Professional Unions 119

    The Shifting Landscape of Professional Unions 120

    The Future of Professional Unions in the Public Sector 124

10. FEDERAL PUBLIC SECTOR UNIONS IN TIMES OF AUSTERITY: LINKING STRUCTURE AND STRATEGIC CHOICE
    (Rosemary Warskett) 126

    Strategic Choice and Union Structure 127

    Looking Back on Austerity in the Federal Public Sector, 1975–2005 130

    Austerity Under the Harper Conservatives 134

    Conclusion 136

REFERENCES 139

ACKNOWLEDGEMENTS 158

CONTRIBUTORS 159

LABOUR IN CANADA SERIES

This volume is part of the Labour in Canada Series, which focuses on assessing how global and national political economic changes have affected Canada's labour movement and labour force as well as how working people have responded. The series offers a unique Canadian perspective to parallel international debates on work and labour in the United States, Great Britain and Western Europe.

Authors seek to understand the impact of governments and markets on working people. They examine the role of governments in shaping economic restructuring and the loss of unionized jobs, as well as how governments promote the growth of low-wage work. They also analyze the impacts of economic globalization on women, minorities and immigrants.

Contributors provide insight on how unions have responded to global labour market deregulation and globalization. They present accessible new research on how Canadian unions function in both the private and public sectors, how they organize and how their political strategies work. The books document recent success stories (and failures) of union renewal and explore the new opportunities emerging as the labour movement attempts to rebuild the economy on sound environmental principles.

Over the past thirty years, the union movement has increasingly been put on the defensive as its traditional tactics of economic and political engagement have failed to protect wages, maintain membership and advance progressive agendas. Yet there has been far too little discussion of how the terrain of Canadian politics has shifted and how this has, in turn, affected the Canadian labour movement. There has also been far too little acknowledgment of working people's attempts to develop new strategies to regain political and economic influence. This series aims to fill these major gaps in public debate.

The volumes are resources that can help unions successfully confront new dilemmas. They also serve to promote discussion and support labour education programs within unions and postsecondary education programs. It is our hope that the series informs debate on the policies and institutions that Canadians need to improve jobs, create better workplaces and build a more egalitarian society.

Series editors
John Peters and Reuben Roth

Labour in Canada series editorial committee:
Marjorie Griffin Cohen, Julie Guard,
Grace-Edward Galabuzi, Joel Harden, Wayne Lewchuk,
Stephanie Ross, Larry Savage, Mercedes Steedman and Erin Weir

PUBLIC SECTOR UNIONS IN THE AGE OF AUSTERITY

Stephanie Ross and Larry Savage

Public sector unions across the advanced capitalist world are under attack. Austerity measures in Greece have led to deep and unprecedented public sector wage cuts and layoffs. Throughout the rest of the European Union, hundreds of thousands of public sector workers have had their wages frozen or have been thrown out of work to pay for an economic crisis that was not of their making. In the United States, the all-out legislative attack in 2011 on public sector unionism in Wisconsin, ironically the first state to allow public sector collective bargaining, and the adoption of "right to work" legislation in 2012 in Michigan, the cradle of American industrial unionism, have justifiably set off alarm bells for unions north of the border.

Like their counterparts around the globe, Canada's public sector unions have been struggling against austerity, privatization, marketization, public-private partnerships, "taxpayer" backlash and restrictions on union rights and freedoms. However, the level and intensity of state-led attacks have reached dizzying heights in recent years. To make matters worse, growing signs of "reverse class resentment" — the idea that working-class people are misdirecting their anger and resentment at union members rather than big business — are increasingly evident (Walkom 2010). Public sector unions are increasingly cast as defenders of sectional rather than the public interest and are castigated when they seek to defend their collective agreements, particularly through strikes and other tactics that interrupt service. If public sector unions are "militant" in the typical mode of industrial unions, most risk public hostility.

Despite these mounting pressures, public sector unions remain central to the overall labour movement, representing a wide and diverse group of workers in public administration, health care, education, police and fire protection, public utilities, social services and municipal government.[1] Despite this significance, public sector unionism is understudied in industrial relations, labour history, labour studies and most social sciences in favour of both craft and industrial unions. The unique status of public sector workers and their unions is widely recognized, given their location in and relationship to public institutions (Johnston 1994: 4). However, the implications of that distinctiveness are narrowly cast.

In the Canadian context, the literature on public sector unionism is usually situated in a discussion of labour relations, collective bargaining, compensation levels, interest arbitration and the right to strike, dominated by a labour relations lens (rather than a political or social movement one).[2] While the broader political context framing public sector labour relations is acknowledged (Gunderson and Hyatt 1996: 244), the ensuing discussion tends to centre on whether it is appropriate for public sector workers to be unionized and bargaining with governments or other publicly funded organizations, the costs of which are "imposed" on the taxpayer, and whether they should be permitted to withdraw their labour.[3] Rarely, however, are public sector unions discussed in terms of their unique *political* features, by which we mean the kinds of claims made, strategies used and practices adopted to engage in power struggles over the place of public sector workers and their contribution to the broader society. The existing literature's concepts and concerns have been unable to capture and adequately analyze the reasons for and implications of this political and ideological distinctiveness. As David Camfield (2005: 56) argues, we need a new theoretical lens that "considers [public sector unions] as a particular kind of working-class movement organization within a historically-specific class formation" rather than simply another labour relations institution. This book seeks to address these gaps by exploring the strategic implications of the unique role of public sector workers and unions and examining the various options available to public sector unions intent on challenging austerity and enhancing public sector union power.

DEFINING THE PUBLIC SECTOR

There is no consensus among labour relations scholars on a precise definition of the public sector. Thompson and Jalette (2009: 406) have defined the public sector as including federal, provincial and municipal governments, Crown corporations and the health-care and education sectors. Peirce and Bentham (2007: 208) have employed a similar working definition but exclude Crown corporations, while McQuarrie's definition (2011: 16) includes Crown corporations but excludes the health-care and education sectors. This book defines the public sector in the widest possible terms as the sector of the economy concerned with the provision, production, distribution and allocation of public goods and services. We thus include para-public organizations[4] like hospitals, schools, universities and Crown corporations as part of the public sector. We also include a chapter on the nonprofit social services sector, which, although technically separate from the public sector, is very much linked. By adopting this broad scope, we are able to better capture the enormous variety of work processes, occupational cultures, political orientations and bargaining strategies that characterize the relationships between public sector workers, their employers, their unions and the publics they serve. These different relationships have implications for the ways public sector unions define the public good, mobilize their members and allies and achieve their goals.

Roughly one out of every five Canadian workers is employed in the broader public sector, and of those, over 70 percent are members of unions. This compares to just 15.9 percent of private sector workers in Canada who belong to unions (Thorpe 2012). The vast majority of all union members in Canada now belong to public sector unions. This was not always the case. In the late 1960s, private sector unionists dominated the labour movement. A number of public sector workers had formed "associations" in the early twentieth century, but these organizations lacked the legal force and militant orientation of bona fide labour unions. In the immediate postwar period, public sector workers watched their private sector counterparts climb the economic ladder at an accelerated pace thanks to the benefits of unionization and collective bargaining. Eager not to be left behind, many public sector workers began to press for their associations to become unions in order to capitalize on the material benefits of collective bargaining. The passage of the *Public Sector Staff Relations Act* (*PSSRA*) in 1967, which extended collective bargaining rights to most federal public service workers, and similar legislation in the provinces, ushered in a new era of impressive public sector union growth in the 1970s. Public sector union growth, however, was not restricted to federal and provincial government employees. The Canadian Union of Public Employees (CUPE) was organizing workers in the para-public sector at an unprecedented rate, as witnessed by the fact that the union's membership increased from 78,317 in 1963, when it was founded, to over 250,000 by 1978 (Ross 2005: 281; Maslove and Swimmer 1980: 135). By 1975, nearly half of all union members in Canada worked in the public sector, and CUPE had become the country's largest union (Heron 2012: 98). As the ranks of private sector unions shrank as a result of globalization, deindustrialization and work restructuring in the 1980s and 1990s, the share of union members belonging to public sector unions grew even more as a result, thus consolidating the dominance of public sector unions within the contemporary Canadian labour movement.

It has been argued that the relative numerical strength and political-ideological orientation of public sector unions explains both the quantitative and qualitative difference in strength of the Canadian labour movement in comparison to its U.S. counterpart (Huxley et al. quoted in Panitch and

Swartz 2003: 146). The relatively higher levels of union density in the Canadian public sector have counterbalanced the decline in private sector union density to a far greater extent than in the US, leading to higher overall unionization levels. However, the more developed and widespread social unionist orientation in public sector unions has also contributed to the qualitative differences between the two movements (Swartz 1993).[5]

There are important strategic implications for the labour movement when a growing majority of union members belongs to public sector unions. Specifically, the overwhelming public sector makeup of organized labour in Canada changes the very nature of the class struggle. Because public sector unionists are not employed by private sector capitalists, their work does not produce surplus value in the traditional manner understood by Marxist scholars. When public sector unionists collectively withdraw their labour, they are not striking a capitalist business but rather the state, and arguably by extension, the public. Indeed, whereas individual capitalist employers risk profit in the event of a strike, some public sector employers may view labour disputes as a method of recouping costs, given that wages tends to be the biggest budget line in public or para-public sector organizations. In addition, many public sector employers are not themselves in direct control of their budgets, and unions must negotiate with them rather than the governments who hold the purse strings.

However, the public sector does play a central role in organizing the social reproduction of the conditions that make capitalist society possible, including the education, availability and dispositions of workers, the provision of collective infrastructure and the maintenance of a "good business climate" (Peck 1996; Naiman 2008: 178). While many social reproductive activities are carried out in the (gendered) private sphere (Bezanson and Luxton 2006), capitalist employers are also dependent on the public sector for the conditions that make profit-making possible. Moreover, as a terrain of struggle on which different classes and social forces battle for their interests, the state has institutionalized other purposes that conflict with those of capital. The labour mobilizations of the mid-twentieth century led to an expansion of social rights, which were operationalized in a welfare state that decommodified important elements of life (Teeple 2000). Elements of the public are thus attached to public services that shield them from the excesses of market discipline and provide them with entitlements based on citizenship rather than their ability to pay for services. As such, the provision — and interruption — of public services matters to various groups but in different ways and with different political dynamics. Given these distinct and contradictory conditions, public sector unions' capacity to exert power in this context is complicated, often forcing them to frame their demands and political activities around defining, protecting and expanding the public good.

UNDERSTANDING PUBLIC SECTOR LABOUR RELATIONS

While public sector and private sector unionists share many workplace concerns over wages, job security and workload, there are also important differences. In his chapter, Bryan Evans explores the political context in which public sector labour relations unfolds and argues that the state's dual role as both legislator and employer presents public sector unions with a unique set of challenges. After reviewing the history of public sector unionism in Canada, Evans analyzes the structural constraints imposed upon public sector unionists in pursuit of workplace justice and makes the case that such workers must politicize the public sector employment relationship in order to fully realize their strategic potential. To be sure, the challenges facing public sector unionists intent on resisting neoliberal employer offensives have been made all the more daunting by sustained and increasingly brutal attacks on public sector union freedoms since the mid 1970s.

Expanded designations of "essential" workers, limits on or the complete removal of the right to strike and the increased use of back-to-work legislation are all manifestations of what Leo Panitch and Donald Swartz have famously termed "permanent exceptionalism" (Panitch and Swartz 2003). Revisiting their earlier work, Panitch and Swartz argue in their chapter that temporary restrictive measures on labour rights have become a permanent fixture in Canadian labour relations, particularly in the public sector. In reviewing the coercive federal and provincial legislation adopted since the turn of the new millennium, they argue that the permanent exceptionalism thesis rings more true today than ever before, notwithstanding nominally pro-union Supreme Court decisions in this period. Panitch and Swartz point to the limitations of judicial-based strategies for defending or enhancing labour's political power, arguing instead for the articulation of common class interests that are capable of mobilizing broad popular support for labour's cause in the political arena. To be sure, this is no small task. In the face of unprecedented neoliberal restructuring, some public sector unions have taken up political strategies that mobilize a wider constituency in support of public services, while others have responded by turning inward, focusing on their own narrow sectional interests in the hope that they might be shielded from the onslaught of austerity.

PUBLIC SECTOR UNION RESPONSES TO NEOLIBERAL AUSTERITY

How public sector unions respond to neoliberalism is one of the central preoccupations of this book. Staring down the real prospect of "right to work" laws and the wholesale removal of the right to strike for certain segments of the public sector will require strategic union responses that are informed by the unique structures and practices of public sector unions. There exists a wide spectrum of public sector union identities and strategies, ranging from the high-profile militancy of unionized postal workers to the low-key diplomacy of unionized senior civil servants. The existence or nonexistence of the right to strike for certain segments of the public sector also influences the character and strategic orientation of specific groups of public sector workers.

We also see a wide variety of electoral political expressions in the public sector, ranging from strict nonpartisanship to active engagement in the New Democratic Party (NDP). In their chapter on electoral politics, Larry Savage and Charles W. Smith demonstrate that the public sector labour movement in Canada has always lacked a unified approach to electoral activity. They further argue that the public sector labour movement's refusal to fully embrace the NDP as an electoral political vehicle can be partially explained by the uncomfortable dual role that social democratic parties play as both allies and employers of public sector workers, especially in times of austerity. This dynamic creates a unique political problem for public sector workers, raising questions about loyalty and independence and stimulating discussion about alternate ways that public sector unions can exert political power.

Today, Canada's public sector unions are at the forefront of anti-austerity struggles, extraparliamentary political action and community coalitions promoting social justice or defending public services. In their respective chapters on union orientations and modes of action, Stephanie Ross and David Camfield both explore the bases for public sector union power in the face of austerity. Ross focuses specifically on the reasons why public sector unions tend to adopt social unionist visions and strategies, even when framing their collective bargaining demands. She locates these tendencies in the fact that public sector unions' power is not primarily economic but rather rests on their capacity to mobilize service recipients and the public as allies against employers. In his chapter, Camfield argues that public sector unions must embrace a social movement mode of unionism as part of an overall process of renewal. Social movement unionism, Camfield argues, is a more radical, militant and democratic form of unionism that holds the greatest potential for building public sector union power. Both point to the way that public sector unions cannot rely merely on the type of unionism prescribed by the postwar labour relations regime, which confines workers to the workplace terrain and the collective bargaining process.

LESSONS FROM PUBLIC SECTOR UNION STRUGGLES

An important part of what shapes union responses and strategies is demographic. The public sector labour movement includes more women and more professional and white-collar workers than its private sector counterpart. Women's significant participation in public sector employment accounts not only for women's rising access to unions over the past forty years but also for the fact that women are now unionized at a higher rate than men (Uppal 2011). Women's greater presence and participation in public sector unions has had a major impact on their internal culture, decision-making and strategic priorities (Heron 2012: 143–147; Kainer 2009; Briskin and McDermott 1993). Moreover, many (though not all) public sector workers are engaged in work that requires them to care for, serve or protect members of the public. These demographic and occupational aspects inform the ways that public sector unions frame their strategic approaches to organizing, collective bargaining and political mobilization.

In her chapter, Donna Baines focuses on the growing nonprofit sector and effectively demonstrates how an "ethos of care" for the populations they serve helps to shape the identities and labour strategies of an overwhelmingly female and increasingly racialized nonprofit workforce. Baines analyzes how nonprofit sector workers have used unions to improve working conditions while simultaneously challenging service cuts to vulnerable populations. Linda Briskin demonstrates in her chapter how nurses' unions have effectively promoted a militant gendered discourse emphasizing patient care in support of their bargaining objectives. This "politicization of caring," which expands the collective bargaining terrain to include the wider public interest, has helped nurses' unions to foster widespread public support for their job actions.

While both Baines and Briskin emphasize gendered aspects of public sector work, Andy Hanson's chapter on teachers' unions and Savage and Michelle Webber's chapter on unions of professional workers focus on the "professional" dimensions of public sector work. Professionalism is a contested terrain and its implications for the character of public sector unionism are indeterminate. It depends on who is using professionalist discourse and to what ends. In the case of teachers, Hanson argues that professionalism has been used in different historical periods to either rally teachers to defend their employment interests or to demobilize them at the bargaining table. Continuing with this theme, Savage and Webber remind us that the language of "professionalism" is not a class-based discourse and can often reinforce rather than challenge class hierarchy. In their case studies of university faculty, federal and provincial civil servants and a range of scientific and technical professionals, Savage and Webber argue that discourses of professionalism can serve to both mobilize and constrain the workplace actions of professional workers, often simultaneously. This dynamic, they argue, is reflected in both the strategies and institutional characteristics of professional unions. While the character of professional unions is certainly changing amid unprecedented neoliberal restructuring, many professional workers continue to embrace their particular union formations, based loosely around notions of occupational prestige while demonstrating little, if any, affinity with the broader working class.

The ever-present problem of sectionalism is also taken up in Rosemary Warskett's chapter, which explores the link between union structure and strategic choice. Warskett juxtaposes two of Canada's largest federal public sector unions, the Public Service Alliance of Canada (PSAC) and the Canadian Union of Postal Workers (CUPW), with a view to demonstrate how different union formations and structures can help produce very different strategic orientations and solidaristic union practices. Ultimately, she concludes that CUPW is better equipped to resist neoliberal reforms in the federal public service because of its more inclusive conception of solidarity, rooted in its organizational structure and in the union's early pivotal battles.

CONCLUSION

The corporate media would have us believe that austerity is the direct result of the wage demands of greedy public sector unions intent on plunging governments of all political stripes deeper into debt without a care for the taxpaying public. While this corporate frame conveniently ignores the role of the financial industry in precipitating the Great Recession that began in 2007, blaming political and economic problems on unionized public sector workers does serve the interests of right-wing politicians and their capitalist allies who, in the name of profit, seek to undermine support for public services and public sector unions.

Canada's public sector unions thus face an uphill battle that will require strategic thinking and modes of action that are rediscovered or altogether untested. The chapters of this book explore the possibilities, limits and contradictions that public sector unions have and will continue to face in defending the employment interests of their members. We offer these insights in the hope they will stimulate discussion and critical debate about the role public sector unions must play in challenging austerity, enhancing the collective power of workers and effectively connecting the interests of public sector workers with those of citizens who desire a more just and equitable public sphere.

Notes

1. Although our focus in this book is on public sector workers, public sector unions do represent a comparatively small number of private sector workers as well. For example, CUPE represents a number of workers in privately-run nursing homes. Conversely, some private sector unions, like the Canadian Auto Workers, represent a comparatively small number of public sector workers, primarily in the health-care sector.
2. For a similar point, see Camfield 2005 and Johnston 1994: 23. Camfield (2005) provides a useful review of existing literature on public sector unions as well as its limits.

3. From early on, debates about public sector workers' unionization were framed in terms of whether it was appropriate for state employees to organize at all and, if yes, whether they should be permitted to bargain the full scope of issues typical in private sector labour relations (Frankel 1962).
4. "Para-public" refers to organizations that rely heavily on state funding but are not directly operated by federal, provincial or municipal governments.
5. Other reasons cited for the differences include the later struggle for public sector collective bargaining rights, which meant that the militant legacy of recognition struggles was still alive when the crisis of the 1970s and neoliberal restructuring began.

1. WHEN YOUR BOSS IS THE STATE
The Paradoxes of Public Sector Work

Bryan Evans

What makes public sector unions different from their private sector counterparts? Of course, for public and private sector workers, the issues negotiated by their unions through collective bargaining are not fundamentally different. Bargaining in both sectors tends to be concerned with the standard issues of wages, benefits, working time, conditions of employment, health and safety and job security (Gunderson, Ponak and Taras 2005: 424). This glosses over one rather commanding difference: the dual role of the state as employer and as sovereign legislator. When your boss is the state, workers' issues and concerns exist within a very different context of power relations. As a purchaser of labour power, the state shares with the private capitalist similar interests in controlling the organization and cost of work, but unlike the capitalist owner, the state possesses the authority to write and enforce laws to suit its objectives.

This chapter is composed of four sections. First, a brief history of the origins of Canadian public sector unions provides an overview of the transition from employee associations to bona fide labour unions and the emergence of a legal framework enabling collective bargaining. The second component traverses the 1970s ascent of neoliberalism and explores how this paradigm shift manifested in public sector labour relations. The third section demonstrates how a distinctly different employer-employee relationship prevails in the public sector and para-state organizations (for example, boards of education, hospitals, universities). Finally, the chapter concludes with a discussion of the potential of public sector struggles to contribute to challenging neoliberalism.

PUBLIC SECTOR UNIONS IN HISTORICAL PERSPECTIVE

The public sector is not a monolithic and homogeneous entity. It is complex and diverse. Consequently, it is impossible to tell one story capable of detailing the important differences in the origin and experiences of individual unions situated in distinctive parts of the public sector. Each government public service union (those representing workers employed directly by the state) possesses a unique history. And distinctions sharpen with unions representing teachers, nurses, hospital workers, postal workers and other employees working in para-state organizations. Accounting for the multitude of political experiences is a tremendous task. Accordingly, we can only generalize and point to examples from these histories that illustrate the general evolution of public sector unionism.

The passage of the *Trade Unions Act* in 1872 by the federal parliament removed the criminal taint on labour unions. However, it did not apply to government workers. Indeed, even to request a wage increase was deemed grounds for termination (Morton 2007: 255). Still, public employees banded together in voluntary associations, the first of which was established in 1889 by postal workers (CUPW 2000). These associations played a consultative role, raising issues related to wages and working conditions for the employers' consideration (Rose 2007: 184). They had no legal or even ideological basis to enforce their claims and relied entirely on employer beneficence. These associations were conservative in every sense: they rejected conflict, allowed managers to associate and avoided any linkage with the labour movement (Peirce and Bentham 2007: 209). By the conclusion of the Second World War, provincial government employees in every province were represented by such associations (Fryer 1995: 347). Labour legislation everywhere, with the exception of Saskatchewan where the pro-union Cooperative Commonwealth Federation governed, excluded public sector workers (save for municipal blue-collar workers) from the right to unionize, bargain or strike. Governments contended that granting union rights to public sector workers would result in disruption and undermine public security (Morton 2007: 25). The implementation in 1944 of Order-in-Council PC 1003, a wartime labour relations regulation issued by the federal cabinet, established a bargaining framework for the private sector, but most workers employed by the state would wait at least another twenty-three years for comparable rights.

Despite this subservient status, there were occasional explosions of militancy suggesting the days of docile associations were numbered. Indeed the first public sector strike was waged in 1918 when letter carriers entered into a ten-day illegal strike that ended with the workers winning a 44-hour week, overtime pay, wage increases, a commitment there would be no retaliation against strikers and a commission of inquiry to investigate working conditions at the post office (CUPW 2000). During the Second World War, municipal government workers established unions and demanded the right to collective bargaining that had been won by municipal manual workers during and after the First World War (Ross 2005; Robinson 1993: 30). Again, in the early 1940s, as unionized blue-collar workers rapidly demonstrated significant workplace gains as a result of collective bargaining, federal and provincial government workers, in far more privileged positions, were coming to the realization that their associations were not as effective as bona fide labour unions (Heron 2012: 95). The British Columbia Government Employees Association (BCGEA) best expressed this emerging militancy. In March 1959, members voted 81 percent in favour of a strike despite having no legal right to do so. The issues were wages but also the right to bargain. And for four hours they did strike before being called off the picket lines under threat from the government (McLean 1979: 74–75). B.C. public servants would wait until 1974 when an NDP government would rewrite the labour code to provide full bargaining rights, including the right to strike, to government workers (BCGEU n.d.).

Labour relations were volatile through the 1960s. Rapid public sector expansion created a large, educated labour force with few workplace rights. The dominant employee association model was inadequate for addressing demands for better working conditions, pay and preserving professional autonomy. The BCGEA hinted at an emerging militancy demanding full rights. Québec public sector and federal postal workers would pick up where the BCGEA had left off in steering public sector workers away from the polite begging of the associations and toward full bargaining rights.

The most significant movement toward establishing a full bargaining regime for all public sector workers was in Québec. Service sector expansion was dramatic in Québec, reaching 58.1 percent of all employment by 1965 and driven by the rapidly growing public sector (Lipsig-Mummé 1980: 131). The creation of this new workforce provided the social base for change. The election in 1960 of a labour-supported Liberal government provided the parliamentary mechanism to pursue reform. The ensuing Quiet Revolution included a commitment to introduce a Labour Code; however, the first draft failed to address the issue of public sector collective bargaining. Threats of a general strike, a wildcat strike by hospital workers and increasingly impatient teachers' associations pressed the government to rewrite the Code. In 1964, a new law emerged covering all Québec public sector workers with the exception of police, firefighters and several other groups of "essential" workers (Morton 2007: 260). Québec thus became the second province, twenty years after Saskatchewan, to provide full collective bargaining rights to most of the public sector.

The outcome of the 1963 federal election was an important factor in placing federal public service working conditions on the policy table. The

Liberals, who formed a minority government, had campaigned on introducing collective bargaining into the public sector (Reynolds 1981: 57). A commission of inquiry appointed by the new government reported in 1965 and recommended a bargaining process leading to arbitration in the event of an impasse but not a right to strike (Morton 2007: 258). But 1965 was as propitious a year for federal workers. In that year, a full third of all strikes, many involving public sector workers with few legal protections, were illegal (Robinson 1993: 30). Rapidly moving events overtook the commission. The most significant of these strikes was waged by postal workers in July 1965, mere days after the commission reported. Low wages, authoritarian management and a culture of patronage within the post office created a work environment brewing militancy (Morton 2007: 260). The strike lasted seventeen days and culminated in a large pay increase, earned public sympathy and a commitment by the government that no reprisals would take place (Reynolds 1981: 59). The federal Liberals passed the *Public Service Staff Relations Act* (*PSSRA*) in March 1965 at the behest of the NDP, who held the balance of power in the House of Commons (Peirce and Bentham 2007: 211–12). Full bargaining rights for federal public servants represented a breakthrough for public sector collective bargaining generally.

By 1975, most public employees had become union members: blue collar and white, those working directly for government and those in the broader public sector such as teachers and nurses (Ponak and Thompson 2005: 423). Membership grew from 183,000 in 1961 to 1.5 million twenty years later. Public sector unionists came to compose 43 percent of all union members by 1981 (Rose 2007: 185).

PUBLIC SECTOR LABOUR RELATIONS IN A NEOLIBERAL ERA

The late 1960s also marked the golden age of Canadian Keynesianism as the federal government implemented cost-sharing initiatives in the fields of health, post-secondary education and social services. That the normalization of collective bargaining in the public sector ran parallel to welfare state expansion is not coincidental. Up to the 1970s, the mixed-market[1] approach of Keynesian economics worked extremely well, helping to usher in a golden era of capitalism characterized by low levels of unemployment, low inflation, expanding consumption and a robust welfare state (Palley 2005). However, the economic turmoil of the mid 1970s challenged Keynesian economics: the postwar political consensus wobbled in the face of stagflation, an unheard of combination of high inflation and high unemployment. This economic crisis opened a political fissure for neoliberalism to emerge and supplant Keynesianism. The result has been thirty-five years of retrenchment. In policy terms, neoliberalism manifests itself in terms of trade liberalization, deregulation, privatization and an erosion of worker protections as well as redistributive programs. In essence, neoliberalism views the state's sole role as one of facilitating "conditions for profitable capital accumulation on the part of both domestic and foreign capital" (Harvey 2005: 7).

For public sector workers, the central characteristic has been the state's turn to coercive means restricting workers' ability to engage in bargaining (Panitch and Swartz 2003). For unions generally, neoliberal policies have diminished "their capacities ... to organize and represent the interests of workers" (Albo and Crow 2005: 12). The overriding capacities of the neo-liberal state to re-engineer the production and delivery of public services and rewrite collective agreements is the central feature shaping public sector labour relations since the mid 1970s. Four stages in this history are discern-ible, but these stages are not discontinuous. Each stage, while expressing distinctive characteristics, shares in common a continuous effort to erode the capacities and rights won by public sector unions (Rose 2004 and 2007; Evans and Albo 2011).

The first stage was concerned with managing inflation and marked a rupture with the previous primary concern with maximizing employment. On October 13, 1975, a three-year program of wage and price controls, the federal Anti-Inflation Program (AIP), was announced. Double-digit inflation at the time was attributed, in part, to wage increases, both public and private, as unions attempted to match the inflation spiral. Most of the provinces soon joined, and wage increases were capped at 8, 6 and 4 percent in each of the next three years (Sargent 2005: 15). Public sector unions responded with unprecedented militancy as strike action increased significantly (Mikkelsen 1998: 506). Canada's first and only national general strike on October 14, 1976, drew a million workers to protest controls. The late 1970s also saw the commencement of a four-decade state offensive against solidaristic and redistributive social policies — most of which had been the result of labour-led struggles. And the federal government again confronted postal workers, jailing their president and threatening back-to-work legislation even before a strike took place (Heron 2012: 112–3).

The second stage, covering the 1980s, continued the policy of constrain-ing inflation and containing free collective bargaining. The key difference demarcating this period from the previous one was the willingness of the state, especially at the provincial level, to roll out legislative interventions that sought to weaken union capacities more permanently. For its part, the federal government imposed the *Public Sector Compensation Restraint Act* (*PSCRA*) in 1982. The *PSCRA* extended the terms of existing collective agreements for two years; capped wage increases to 6 and 5 percent for two years; prohibited strikes and access to arbitration; precluded negotiation of even nonmonetary issues; and allowed the government to roll back settlements exceeding the cap (Rose 2004: 237). Six provinces adopted controls modelled on this while the remaining provinces adopted some form of restraint (Peirce and Bentham 2007: 213). Several responded more aggressively. Ontario, for example, imposed a one-year ban on public sector strikes (Morton 2007: 32). Québec's PQ government sought a 20 percent wage cut, suspended the right to strike and introduced legislation removing job security provisions (Heron 2012: 114). The PQ's anti-union offensive demonstrated that a labour-friendly party in government was no guarantee that workers would be protected. The Québec labour movement responded with a short general strike in 1982. British Columbia's right-wing Social Credit government sought to weaken the organizing and bargaining power of public and private sector workers by tabling twenty-six bills with its 1982 budget, effectively suspending collective bargaining (Heron 2012: 115). To add insult to injury, B.C. public sector workers faced both a wage freeze and a target to reduce government employment by 25 percent (Peirce and Bentham 2007: 214). In response, B.C. workers, together with civil society social movements, united in the Operation Solidarity Coalition to resist the provincial government's assault on labour. The central union leadership was not convinced a province-wide general strike was an appropriate strategy. Ultimately, they quietly negotiated the so-called "Kelowna Accord," which effectively ended organized labour's participation in the movement. It was not much of an "accord" as the government maintained in whole or in part nearly all of its anti-labour legislative agenda. An entire "movement had been bartered" for a few exceptionally modest concessions from the government (Palmer 1987: 78). However, this agreement created deep and incapacitating divisions within the coalition[2] (Richmond and Shields 2011: 226–7) and it ultimately dissolved. The divisions created an opportunity in 1984 and 1987 for the B.C. government to pass new, even more far-reaching anti-union laws, which included restrictions on the right to strike, the creation of strike-free economic zones and the establishment of an industrial relations commissioner empowered to prevent strikes and impose settlements (Morton 2007: 323). Several provinces followed B.C.'s lead, including Alberta, Saskatchewan, Manitoba, Québec and Newfoundland, all of which passed legislation to limit the ability of public sector unions to engage in free collective bargaining and to strike (Heron 2012: 115).

The 1990s, the third stage, was characterized by sustained state efforts to suppress public sector wages but justified as part of the battle to shrink state debt as growing budget deficits supplanted inflation as the overarching concern of fiscal policy.[3] Wage restraint was combined with other strategies, including shrinking the public sector and restructuring the production and delivery of public services (Warrian 1996). Unilateral legislative intervention by the state continued to be a favoured weapon (Rose 2004: 274–5). The focus on deficit and debt created an ideological space for a serious reconsideration of public services delivery, including a turn to privatization, public-private partnerships and contracting out (Haiven et al. 2005: 24–5). High union density in the Canadian public sector, ranging from a low of 69.5 percent in Ontario to a high of 81.4 percent in Québec (Statistics Canada 1997–2011), presented an obstacle to unfettered restructuring. Nonetheless, the "balance" of political and economic power had profoundly shifted.

Table 1 Public Sector Union Density, 1997–2011

	1997	2004	2011	Change, 1997–2011	% Change, 1997–2011
Canada	74.66	75.48	74.06	-0.60	-0.81
NFLD & LAB	77.94	75.99	77.09	-0.84	-1.08
PEI	74.03	80.56	78.04	4.01	5.42
NS	66.53	72.22	73.95	7.42	11.15
NB	71.06	73.57	71.51	0.45	0.64
QC	81.53	81.94	81.43	-0.10	-0.12
ON	69.69	70.71	69.54	-0.15	-0.22
MB	77.01	77.34	76.79	-0.22	-0.29
SK	76.70	75.62	75.28	-1.42	-1.85
AB	70.00	69.63	70.07	0.07	0.10
BC	79.44	81.44	75.36	-4.08	-5.13

Source: Calculated from Labour Force Survey data provided by the Labour Statistics Division, Statistics Canada

Graph 1 Legislative Interventions – All Jurisdictions, 1982–2012

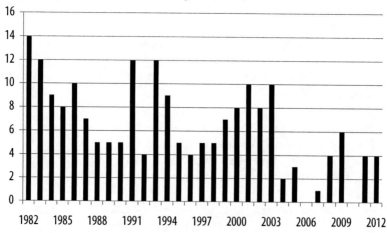

A review of provincial government interventions through the decade confirms that legislative intervention had become an accepted and reliable default where "free" negotiations failed to deliver governments' desired results.

In 1991, the Newfoundland government imposed a one-year wage freeze and then extended that freeze for an additional three years. Nova Scotia adopted similar measures. PEI rolled back public sector compensation by 8.5 percent. In Manitoba, wages were frozen for one year. This was followed in 1993 by legislation requiring public sector workers to take ten unpaid days per year for the next two years. In Saskatchewan a five-year agreement was reached after a series of rotating strikes by public service unions. Modest wage adjustments were followed by back-to-work legislation for resisting health-care workers. Alberta cut public expenditures by 20 percent over 1994–1997. Provincial government employees took a 5 percent pay reduction through unpaid days and a wage freeze (Peirce and Bentham 2007: 216–9). In Ontario, macroeconomic and ideological convergence fundamentally reshaped the terrain of debate. In that decade, the social democratic NDP was succeeded in government by the neoliberal populist Progressive Conservatives, and both parties framed public sector workers and public services as the problem. The NDP's Social Contract austerity program and the Conservatives' anti-union Common Sense Revolution platform together presented a coherent and continuous thread of neoliberal restructuring. Only B.C.'s NDP government broke the pattern with a "social accord" with health-care sector workers,

Graph 2 Number of Work Stoppages, Canada, 1980–2011

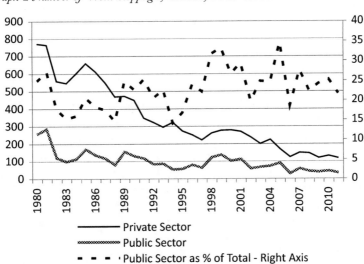

Private Sector
Public Sector
Public Sector as % of Total - Right Axis

Source: Calculated from data obtained from the Workplace Information Directorate, Labour Program, Human Resources and Social Development Canada

which avoided job loss by instituting workforce reductions through attrition, early retirement and reductions in working time (Fryer 1995: 361–3).

As Canada entered the twenty-first century, militancy increased in the early part of the decade as the escalating trend in strike action indicates. Unions sought to make up for years of lost ground, but the state unrelentingly pursued hard bargaining. In 2005, the Québec Liberal government introduced legislation imposing a two-year wage freeze and restricted wage increases thereafter to 2 percent. Moreover, a menacing anti-strike provision impaired union resistance. The combined effect of five years of frozen wages followed by increases below the rate of inflation resulted in a decline in real wages of 4 percent (Mandel 2010). This signaled a fundamental shift in governments' approach to labour relations: sustained fiscal restraint now became a permanent feature of twenty-first-century public management. For governments, dealing sternly with unions was often good for the polling numbers. Thus, for the government-employer, reforming collective bargaining was essential to sustaining an environment where the cost of providing reasonable public services would not require higher taxes. The new normal, the foundations of which had been built over the previous thirty-five years of neoliberal praxis, would be sustained by one means or another. The late 1990s saw a return to negotiations but also no end to governments' willingness to engage coercive tactics and measures and public sector employers' preparation to withstand strikes. While unions entered bargaining expecting to catch up on the previous decade's losses (as had been common in previous periods of restraint), governments' objective was to consolidate prior victories and continue restructuring (Rose 2004: 277). Despite a spike in strike action, public sector unions were unable to make significant improvements (Rose 2007: 187).

The success of governments' adoption of compensation restraint as a permanent feature of fiscal policy is evident. In the first decade of the twenty-first century, average public sector wage increases were 1.5 percent (Statistics Canada, CANSIM Tables 2780008 and v36393). This fell well below the 2.1 percent inflation rate for the same period (Bank of Canada n.d.). Of course, the national average masks the unevenness in the provincial scene where public sector workers experienced deeper erosions in purchasing power. Workers in eight provinces finished the decade with average wage increases below the national average for 2001–2011 (Statistics Canada, CANSIM Tables 2780008 and v36393).

The fourth and current stage began with the 2010 budget cycle. The fiscal and economic context has its origins in the U.S. mortgage market crisis of 2007, which by autumn 2008 descended into a general crisis of the global financial system. By 2009, the crisis was reaching deep into the "real" economy. The ensuing rescue strategies prevented general economic collapse.

However, political elites were designing exit strategies even as expansionary measures were being announced. As the crisis unfolded, a new phase of political contestation emerged over which social groups would pay the price for the crisis. In Canada this began with the 2010 federal budget, which entailed a plan for exit from deficit financing and a return to balanced budget orthodoxy. For the provinces the exit was uneven. In 2009, the ten provinces collectively ran the largest provincial deficit in history at $48.2 billion. This equals 3.2 per cent of provincial GDP (Conference Board of Canada 2010). For some of the provinces, especially Ontario and Québec, exiting deficit would require reconsidering public service delivery.

All provinces have restricted expenditure growth to 2 percent per year or less, cut or frozen operational budgets and constrained compensation. Nova Scotia and Ontario have introduced a high income earners tax and Ontario and Manitoba have postponed corporate tax cuts (TD Economics 2010b: 7). Québec's was the most aggressive attack on public services. For those working for the province, the future would include a four-year pay freeze, a shrinking of the number of public sector workers and the closure or amalgamation of thirty public agencies (Québec Ministry of Finance 2010).

Austerity and the threat of broad legislative intervention into public sector collective bargaining also returned with Ontario's 2010 budget. A seven-year period of austerity, extending to 2017–18, was forecast and would conclude only with a return to fiscal balance. In the process, Ontario's public sector would shrink from 19.2 percent of GDP in 2010 to 15.5 percent in 2017–18 (TD Economics 2010a: 1). Moreover, a massive privatization of public assets was suggested (Evans and Albo 2010: 22).

That 2010 budget introduced the *Public Sector Compensation Restraint to Protect Public Services Act*, which imposed a two-year wage freeze on all nonunion public sector staff and subsequently was extended. The crisis, the government explained, "opened a significant fiscal gap" causing revenues to decline and expenditures to rise as stimulus spending rolled out (Ontario Ministry of Finance 2010). If a balanced budget was to be achieved by 2017–18, no more than 0.7 percent annually remained to finance improvements in compensation (ibid.). The budget also called for a social dialogue with unions representing 700,000 broader public sector workers with a view to negotiate a two-year wage freeze (Ontario Ministry of Finance 2010). This process was abandoned after several months (Evans 2011).

Setting a more threatening tone, the 2011 budget announced the Commission on Reform of Public Services to be headed by TD Bank economist Don Drummond. The commission's report, delivered in early 2012, recommended a wide range of market-driven prescriptions, including massive privatization and significant expansion of contracting out (Nesbitt and Stevens 2012). However, the Liberals shifted their deficit reduction strategy to more clearly focus on wage controls and the suspension of collective bargaining. In the autumn of 2012, Ontario's Liberals intervened directly to seize control of bargaining throughout the broader Ontario public sector. Bill 115, the *Putting Students First Act, 2012*, froze compensation and centralized decision-making over the terms and conditions of employment in Ontario's primary and secondary education systems. The proposed *Protecting Public Services Act*[4] would have extended the pay freeze to unionized public sector workers, terminating only when the deficit was eliminated.In both instances, ministers were empowered to act unilaterally on all labour relations matters, including issuing back-to-work orders, thus avoiding the legislature.

With Canada now in its fourth decade of neoliberalism, we can look back and make several observations about public sector labour relations. Contrary to what is often said, public sector workers have not been protected or privileged through this process. Whether the focus of government policy has been combating inflation or state debt, public sector workers' incomes, working conditions, indeed their very employment, are targeted. Public sector workers are called upon to compensate for the state's refusal to democratize public services delivery, consider expanding the role of the public sector in key parts of the economy and in social provision or return to a progressive and enforced regime of taxation. Since the 1960s, we see that workers can rely only on their autonomous capacities to struggle and resist attacks on their rights, whether in striking illegally to force federal and provincial governments to respond to their grievances and expand collective bargaining rights or in creating broad coalitions between labour and social movements to mobilize against neoliberal social policy. Where these strategies fail, the result is always the state's return to coercion.

WHAT MAKES WORKING FOR THE STATE DIFFERENT?

What makes working for the state different from working for a privately owned transnational corporation? The foregoing historical narrative tells the essential story. As state workers, public sector unions and their members have their collective rights and capacities regulated directly by the state. And, in the contemporary era, that state is neoliberal in role and purpose. The canvassing of history here illustrates explicitly that "public sector unions have been shaped by the form of that state power" (Camfield 2005: 64). The obvious answer is that state work, unlike that in the private sector, takes place within a context where the economic and political spheres are unified. As such, the state, through its role as employer, possesses the material capability to appropriate the labour power of its workforce and to deploy coercive instruments, including legislation, enforcement and prosecution, to impose discipline. The duality within capitalism, "appropriation and coercion" (Wood 1995: 30), is reunited within the state. Notwithstanding the liberal democratic image of the state as neutral arbitrator, the reality is that the state has an interest in establishing policies that serve the interests of capital as well as its own (Godard 2005: 248).

A second dimension of the state's distinctiveness is found in the 1940s origins of the Canadian labour relations regime. The bargaining regime set out with PC 1003, and replicated in provincial legislation, applied primarily to private sector workplaces. Certain groups of broader public sector workers such as municipal and school board employees were covered, but some provincial legislation enabled their employers to opt out (Crean 1995: 44). The model's essence was that unions were legally limited to bargaining with only one local employer over local workplace conditions. This further meant that disputes and any actions stemming from such were to be confined to that local workplace. In other words, disputes could not spill over into secondary pickets or solidarity strikes, thus impinging on the business of other employers. Strike action would be required to singularly target the local employer and confined to the settlement of workplace economic issues, not to achieve political objectives. For public sector unions the legal and ideological implications would be significant. The 1940s legal framework constructed unions as organizations representing the narrow economic interests of their members and prohibited demands of a fundamentally political type. In other words, "collective economic power is not to be used in such a way as to affect the allocation and raising of funds" for public services (Glasbeek 2009: 13).

In the public sector, this ideological feature of the labour relations regime circumscribes the parameters of bargaining in several ways. The political executive claims sole legitimacy to act in the interest of all citizens and exercises this role through authoritative policy decisions. Conversely, unions do not possess such political legitimacy and are instead rhetorically and ideologically defined as an economic special interest. Thus, public sector labour relations can be framed as a conflict between the sectional demands of the unions against the policy-making role of government as the guardian of broad public interests (Swimmer and Thompson 1995: 2–3). The counterpoint for public workers is their capacity to build strategic alliances with public services users and frame demands in the public interest. Doing so "places a potent political edge" on the claims made by those who produce and deliver public services (Johnston 1994: 11).

In addition, the 1960s expansion of collective bargaining rights to a broader cross-section of public sector workers was limited. Governments deem various public services as essential where such workers are prevented from participating in strike action. In addition, the record demonstrates governments readily suspend collective bargaining and unilaterally set the terms of employment. This dual role of the state, as sovereign legislator and employer, distinguishes it explicitly from a private employer.

A third dimension is the state's relative autonomy from market forces. When a private employer confronts a strike, they may contend with loss of market share, as competitors move in to fill production gaps and, stemming from this, loss of revenue, as sales in the absence of a stockpile diminish. For both the state and most broader public sector employers, these factors do not exist or are minimal. Moreover, from a financial perspective, a strike may in fact be positive for a state employer as workers are not paid and savings accrue to the state (Peirce and Bentham 2007: 224). And fourth, as canvassed broadly above, those employed by the public sector, the services it delivers, its political and economic purposes, have all been subject to an increasingly intense assault of a vituperative ideological nature.

Exploring the distinct nature of public sector work thus brings into sharp relief issues of class power and the politics through which that power is exercised. In response, Canadian public sector unions are reframing the debate away from questions of compensation and instead focusing on questions of inequality and redistribution. But a cross-union and popular coalition opposing neoliberal austerity has yet to emerge, and whether it will emerge remains an open question. However, the history of public sector unions demonstrates that only by politicizing, which is to say, broadening the contest between public workers and the state can meaningful victories be achieved.

Notes

1. This is characterized by a dominant private sector supported by public policies and programs including selective state ownership.
2. The Solidarity movement was composed of two basic components: a broad coalition of civil society organizations and social movements and trade unions affiliated to the B.C. Federation of Labour. The Kelowna Agreement failed to address the issues raised by the civil society groups, and labour did not consult with the civil society wing of the coalition on whether to accept or not. Consequently, the civil society wing felt betrayed.
3. Between 1988 and 1996, aggregate provincial debt grew from 24 to 37 percent of GDP (Swimmer 1995: 3).
4. With Premier Dalton McGuinty's prorogation of the legislature, the Act was not introduced for a vote by members of the legislature and consequently did not become law.

2. THE CONTINUING ASSAULT ON PUBLIC SECTOR UNIONS

Leo Panitch and Donald Swartz

The first great capitalist crisis of the twenty-first century, which began in the summer of 2007 and five years later was still very much in train, called into question some three decades of neoliberal policies. Indeed, many held that we were about to witness the revival of some form of Keynesianism in a replay of the 1930s. Ultimately, the labour movement and the left generally failed to intervene in a meaningful way, giving capital and the state the time to recover their balance. Any talk of Keynesianism disappeared as states embraced austerity in order to shift the burden of crisis onto the backs of working people. Part and parcel of this strategy was a major assault on workers' rights, led by a flurry of federal back-to-work legislation depriving postal workers, Air Canada workers and CP Rail workers of the rights to bargain and strike (Bronskill 2011; Deveau 2012; Lu 2011).

This assault on workers' collective rights is nothing new, however. Indeed, just as the rights of Canadians as citizens, including freedom of association, were being constitutionally enshrined in the early 1980s, the collective rights of Canadian workers were under assault. Although Prime Minister Pierre Trudeau (1974: 336) himself had written twenty-five years earlier that "if the right to strike is suppressed or seriously limited, the trade union movement becomes nothing more than one institution among many in the service of capitalism," it was his government's introduction of wage control legislation in June 1982 — the same year after freedom of association was constitutionally enshrined in Canada — that led to more than one million workers temporarily losing their rights to bargain and strike for a two-year period.[1]

The Trudeau government's actions exemplified the Canadian state's increasing reliance on coercion relative to consent in managing the relationship between capital and labour (Panitch and Swartz 1984, 2003). This shift, underway since the mid 1970s, was primarily characterized by selective and ad hoc suspensions of the rights to bargain and strike for particular groups of workers for a specific period of time. As the temporary measures piled up, Canada entered a new era we termed "permanent exceptionalism," sustained by the Supreme Court's ruling in the 1987 *Labour Trilogy* decisions that the guarantee of freedom of association in the Canadian Charter of Rights and Freedoms (the Charter) did not encompass workers' rights to bargain or strike.

This chapter begins with a reprise of the history of permanent exceptionalism in the last quarter of the twentieth century, before turning to more recent developments. Notwithstanding the Supreme Court rulings of the past decade, exceptionalism has proved no less permanent in the new millennium and, in the context of the current global economic crisis, may even be in the process of being taken to a new level. We conclude with some reflections on the labour movement's response.

FROM CONSENT TO COERCION

The Trudeau government's 1982 wage control legislation came at the beginning of what has come to be known as the era of neoliberalism. However, the roots of permanent exceptionalism can be traced back to the mid 1970s as part of the crisis of the postwar Keynesian order. The wage militancy that emerged in the 1960s under conditions of full employment, reinforced by the long overdue breakthrough of public sector unionism and the rise of social movements, restricted profits, fuelled inflation and contributed to a fiscal crisis of the state. Labour in all advanced capitalist countries had become stronger in the postwar period, but so had capital, as reflected in the spread of multinational corporations and the growing mobility of finance (Panitch and Gindin 2012: chap. 6).

In the Canadian context, the growing frequency of back-to-work legislation made the shift from consent to coercion most apparent. As Table 1 below shows, there were a mere three instances of back-to-work legislation by the federal and provincial governments combined in the 1950s. During the 1960s this number rose to thirteen and to over forty during the late 1970s.

The ensuing two decades provided substantial evidence that this "temporary" removal of labour rights was not a momentary aberration but a lasting shift. Through the 1980s there were forty-nine instances of back-to-work legislation, more than had been imposed in the 1970s. This occurred despite the existence of wage controls legislation suspending the right to strike for federal and many provincial public sector workers for several of those years. At the same time, the legislation became even more coercive. Governments increasingly imposed the terms of new collective agreements and/or set limits on what arbitrators could award. Reflecting these much more onerous terms, penalties for noncompliance escalated substantially, both for unions as institutions as well for individual members. For example, in the case of Bill C-86, which brought an end to a 1987 postal strike, the legislation went

Table 2 Back-to-Work Measures 1950–2012

Year	Federal	Provincial	Total	Annual Average
1950–54	1	0	1	0.2
1955–59	1	1	2	0.4
1960–64	2	1	3	0.6
1965–69	2	8	10	2.0
1970–74	4	12	16	3.4
1975–79	6	19	25	5.0
1980–84	1	21	22	4.4
1985–89	5	22	27	5.4
1990–94	5	7	12	2.4
1995–99	4	9	13	2.6
2000–04	0	20	20	4.0
2005–09	1	3	4	0.8
2010–12 (Sept.)	4	3	7	2.6

Sources: Compiled from data supplied by the Federal-Provincial Relations Branch, Labour Canada; Human Resources and Development Canada, Labour Program, 1993–94 to 1999–2000; Canadian Foundation for Labour Rights. Figures include both legislation and orders-in-council.

so far as to suppress the right of union members to elect their own leaders by prohibiting any union officer convicted of violating the law from holding office in the union for five years (Panitch and Swartz 2003: 90).

These "temporary" suspensions of trade union rights were increasingly accompanied by avowedly permanent ones. During the 1980s, the federal government as well as nine of the ten provinces introduced permanent restrictions, the most common designating workers as "essential" and thus deprived of their right to strike. But measures that placed new restrictions on the scope of bargaining and/or the ability of workers to form or maintain unions were enacted in several jurisdictions, most notably B.C., Alberta, Newfoundland and Québec (Panitch and Swartz 2003: 253) As the new restrictions on organizing suggest, unions in the private sector were not exempt from the state's turn to coercion, but it remains the case that public sector workers bore the brunt of the assault.

PERMANENT EXCEPTIONALISM AND THE CHARTER

As noted above, the turn toward permanent exceptionalism in the early 1980s coincided with the constitutional entrenchment of the Charter of Rights and Freedoms. As is typical of liberal democratic constitutional discourse, the Charter was silent on whether freedom of association included the rights to bargain and strike. Despite the labour movement's failure to intervene in the debate leading up to the adoption of the Charter (Savage 2008a), unions could hardly ignore the possibility that it would make some difference in blunting the gathering neoliberal assault.

The main question was how narrowly the courts would interpret the Charter rather than whether they would use it to provide substantial new protection for workers' rights to bargain and to strike. Notably, the initial judicial responses were anything but coherent. In the 1983 *Broadway Manor* case, the Ontario High Court unanimously ruled that Ontario's *Inflation Restraint Act*, which extended collective agreements beyond their termination, was unconstitutional. Echoing Trudeau's words some fifty-five years earlier, Justice Galligan argued that:

> Freedom of association must include freedom to engage in conduct which is reasonably consonant with the lawful objectives of the association ... If [workers] are not free to take such lawful steps that they see as reasonable to advance their interests, including bargaining and striking, then as a practical matter their association is barren and useless. (*SEIU Local 204 v. Broadway Manor* 1983: 409)

Notwithstanding these strong words, the ruling was much less of a victory than it appeared. The court found that the Act as a whole was constitutional, ruling that only those parts of the Act that froze the pattern of union organization and restricted bargaining on nonmonetary issues were unconstitutional.

Nonetheless, it was apparent that the Charter and the assault on labour rights in the context of the crisis had upset the balance of Canadian jurisprudence. A judgement limiting permanent exceptionalism to temporary wage restraint was significant as it called into question the range of restrictions on public sector workers' union rights that existed in most jurisdictions. In Alberta, where certain public sector workers were still denied the right to strike entirely, the Lougheed Conservative government immediately announced it would use the notwithstanding clause to ensure this remained the case and at the same time asked the Alberta Court of Appeal for an advisory opinion as to the constitutionality of the relevant Acts. The court responded with a judgement that directly contradicted the *Broadway Manor* ruling, asserting that prohibiting strikes and imposing compulsory arbitration simply did not constitute a meaningful restriction on freedom of association (Alberta Court of Appeal 1984).

The absence of consensus in these and other judicial rulings as to whether freedom of association encompassed freedom to bargain and strike meant that it would be left to the Supreme Court to provide some coherence. On April 9, 1987, in its famous *Trilogy* ruling, the majority ruled that freedom of association did not encompass the rights to bargain and strike. The majority decision, written by Justice Le Dain, drew a sharp distinction between the purpose of association and the activities undertaken in its pursuit and asserted that the latter are merely creations of legislation and thus not subject to constitutional protection. Tellingly, Justice McIntyre supported the majority decision with the observation that the issues before the Court were the outcome of "great pressures to reassess the traditional approaches to ... questions of labour law and policy" that had resulted from "changes in the Canadian national economy." And he went on:

> To intervene in that dynamic process at this early stage by implying constitutional protection for the right to strike ... could go far towards freezing the development of labour relations and curtailing the process of evolution necessary to meet the changing circumstances. (*Reference Re Public Service Employee Relations Act* 1987: para. 182)

It was precisely these changing circumstances that had by the 1980s given rise to neoliberalism, defined in terms of free mobility of capital, free trade, the ascendancy of financial capital and the spread of commodification into every aspect of social life. This was consolidated in the 1990s when the Chrétien Liberal government embraced the North American Free Trade Agreement and brought deficit reduction to the top of the economic agenda. Finance Minister Paul Martin's first budget, apart from extending a wage freeze on federal public sector employees by two years, began a process of offloading services to the provinces with major implications for the continuation of permanent exceptionalism in the twenty-first century. The government also passed no less than three pieces of back-to-work legislation in its first two years in office and went on to legislate both the Canadian Union of Postal Workers (CUPW) and the Public Service Alliance of Canada (PSAC) back to work before the decade was over (Panitch and Swartz 2003: 247).

All this took place despite the fact that the profitability and inflation crisis of the 1970s was fully over. Indeed, pulled by the dynamism of U.S. capitalism through the decade, overall growth rates were relatively robust in Canada during the 1990s (Panitch and Gindin 2012: chap. 7). Nonetheless, the 1990s witnessed further assaults on unions, with Ontario at the forefront. First, the NDP government (like so many other social democratic parties) panicked in the face of the growth of the provincial deficit in the wake of the 1991 recession and unveiled its infamous Social Contract attacking the rights of the province's public sector workers. This in turn opened the way for the Mike Harris-led Conservatives and their right-wing "Common Sense Revolution." In addition to cutting welfare rates by 21.6 percent, the Conservatives fundamentally rewrote the province's labour laws, repealing the NDP's progressive reforms and creating new obstacles to unionization (Panitch and Swartz 2003: 189–193). In Québec, several thousand public sector workers were deprived of their right to strike by being declared "essential," while in Manitoba, government employees and teachers faced new restrictions on their bargaining rights. Finally, in Alberta, the rules governing certification and arbitration were revised so as to create new obstacles to workers' ability to exercise their rights to organize and bargain. By the end of the decade, new permanent restrictions on workers' union rights were also on the books in every Maritime province as well (Panitch and Swartz 2003: 253).

Instances of back-to-work legislation did decline in the 1990s relative to the 1980s, partly due to the existence of legislated wage freezes for much of the time in many jurisdictions. But the decline also reflected the success of the developments that shifted the balance of class forces in favour of capital during the 1980s, evident in the steady decline in strike activity that began in the early 1980s and continued through the 1990s. Indeed, by the end of the 1990s, the frequency of strikes was down to around three hundred per year, comparable to that prior to the upsurge in the mid 1960s (Panitch and Swartz 2003: 244).

PERMANENT EXCEPTIONALISM IN THE TWENTY-FIRST CENTURY

The arrival of the twenty-first century brought no relief from permanent exceptionalism; any sign that workers might use the right to strike to defend their interests prompted new coercive measures. Between 2000 and 2004, various provincial governments enacted twenty back-to-work measures, a very large proportion of which came in the first three years of the new millennium and were targeted at workers in the health and education sectors. This spate of back-to-work measures was the inheritance of the offloading of public services to the provinces by the federal Liberal governments of the 1990s. While no back-to-work measures were passed by the federal government during this period, the federal *Public Service Modernization Act* of 2003 revised the definition of essential service so as to increase the number of public sector workers without the right to strike (PSAC 2011). Concerns over provincial deficits were now further fuelled by the fears of the bond markets regarding the capacity of governments to repay their debts.

The frequency with which governments resorted to temporary suspensions of union rights declined somewhat after 2003, but there was no mistaking their repressiveness. In 2004, the Newfoundland and Labrador government passed what was arguably the harshest piece of back-to-work legislation in Canada, freezing wages for the first two years of a four-year contract, with the union liable for fines of $250,000 per day, and members of up to $25,000 per day and/or dismissal, for disobeying the legislation (Zajc 2004). In Québec, the Charest government called an emergency session of the National Assembly in December 2005 to pass Bill 142, imposing a seven-year agreement on public sector workers — the longest suspension of collective bargaining rights in Canadian history (Fudge 2011).

The arrival of the new millennium was also marked by the imposition of far-reaching permanent restrictions on workers' rights in several jurisdictions. In Québec, the government passed Bills 7 and 8 in 2003, removing the right to unionize from those providing child care and youth services in their homes (CFLR 2012), while Bills 30 and 31 imposed a wholesale amalgamation of bargaining units in the health sector (effectively forcing many workers to change unions) and expanded employers' right to contract out work (MacPherson 2003; Dougherty 2003). In the Prairie provinces, the assault stretched from the Klein government's Bill 27, which eliminated the right to strike for health-care workers in 2003 (Cryderman 2003; Olsen 2003), to Saskatchewan, where the newly elected Saskatchewan Party government passed the *Public Service Essential Services Act*, which, in the absence of agreement between the two parties, gave the employer the right to designate as essential whatever services and individuals it deemed necessary (Graham 2008; Smith 2011; Saskatchewan Court of Queen's Bench 2012).

The most far-reaching and shocking of the permanent restrictions took place in 2002 in B.C., where the Liberal government, having already passed two back-to-work measures against teachers' unions in the previous year, introduced Bills 27 and 28, which repealed the teachers' existing contract and replaced it with one imposed by a government-appointed arbitrator. The Liberals followed up with Bill 29, which literally rewrote the collective agreement imposed on hospital workers the previous year, rolling back their wages, eliminating existing protections from contracting out, allowing the government to eliminate or transfer services without consultation and cutting the rights of existing workers to retraining and placement (Camfield 2006). The B.C. government then moved on to a reactionary overhaul of employment standards, removing the requirement for employers to post a statement of labour rights in the workplace. In 2003, the *Health Partnerships Act* prohibited workers from negotiating limits on contracting out, including successor rights in the health sector. Also in 2003, the government adopted Bill 95, ordering striking BC Ferries workers back to work and followed up a year later by passing Bill 37 in order to end a strike involving 43,000 workers in long-term care facilities.

In the fall of 2005, as negotiations with the school board association once again reached an impasse, B.C. teachers threatened an illegal strike. The Liberals responded by immediately introducing and passing Bill 12 on October 3, which imposed a wage freeze by extending the existing contract until June 2006. Teachers followed through with their threat of an illegal strike on October 7, defying court orders to return to work and forbidding the union to provide strike pay to its members (Palmer 2005; Steffenhagen and Fowlie 2005). Teachers' defiance compelled the government to appoint a mediator who brokered an agreement ending the strike on October 24.

This was one of the few instances in which workers actually fought repressive legislation through direct action. Overwhelmingly, the unions' response had been to comply and then appeal to the courts and/or work to change the government in the next election.

LABOUR RIGHTS AND THE COURTS

In light of the *Trilogy* ruling and other similar ones in the 1980s, the unions had essentially abandoned their efforts to take similar restrictive legislation to the courts in the 1990s. But as we have seen, these were not the only coercive measures they faced, and the unions continued to appeal to the courts against other legislation damaging workers' rights and even enjoyed some success in doing so. In fact, once the crisis of the 1970s had been resolved, the courts began to acknowledge the contradiction between the Charter and the assault on labour rights.

The opening at the Supreme Court first appeared in 1999 with a positive ruling in favour of Kmart workers' freedom of expression (*UFCW v. Kmart* 1999). This was followed by the *Dunmore* decision in 2001, which ruled that the Ontario government's exclusion of agricultural workers from the province's collective bargaining regime was unconstitutional on the grounds that those too vulnerable to exercise the right of freedom of association on their own needed government intervention to secure it on their behalf (*Dunmore v. Ontario* 2001). Although the Court reiterated that freedom of association did not include the rights to bargain or strike, and hence this protection did not require such workers come under the *Ontario Labour Relations Act* (Smith 2012), it was notable that in the following year, the Court overturned a previous decision by ruling in *RWDSU v. Pepsi* that secondary picketing was a form of free expression that should be treated the same as other nonlabour forms of expression.

Such rulings renewed unions' hope that the courts could indeed protect them. They lost no time turning to the courts in the wake of the passage of Bill 29 in B.C.[2] The Supreme Court's *B.C. Health Services* ruling on the constitutionality of Bill 29 in June 2007 appeared to vindicate those hopes, as it dismissed the reasoning in the 1987 *Trilogy* decisions and instead found that the Charter's "guarantee of freedom of association protects the capacity of members of labour unions to engage in collective bargaining on workplace issues" (*B.C. Health Services* 2007: Section 2[d]).

This ruling was widely — and rather incautiously — interpreted as having finally secured labour's right to collective bargaining under the Charter. But expectations that this ruling would halt or reverse the assault on union rights rested on a misunderstanding of the Court's use of the term "collective bargaining." Writing for the majority, justices McLachlin and LeBel made a distinction between a procedure and its substantive outcome. In the context of collective bargaining, formulating demands and discussing them with employers are procedures and collective agreements a substantive outcome.

> Section 2(*d*) does not guarantee the particular objectives sought through this associational activity. However, it guarantees the process through which those goals are pursued. It means that employees have the right to unite, to present demands to health sector employers collectively and to engage in discussions in an attempt to achieve workplace-related goals. Section 2(*d*) imposes corresponding duties on government employers to agree to meet and discuss with them. (*B.C. Health Services* 2007: para. 89)

This right, as the Court made clear, does not entail any specific process or legal framework of collective bargaining. In other words, what the Court meant by collective bargaining then was merely some sort of "consultative" process; it did not encompass dispute resolution mechanisms, such as conciliation or arbitration, let alone the right to strike, collective agreements or procedures for enforcing them that are part and parcel of most understandings of what collective bargaining entails.

Even this sort of consultative process would not always be necessary. In order to violate Section 2(d), any government measure undertaken without consultation

> must be substantial ... the intent or effect must seriously undercut or undermine the activity of workers joining together to pursue the common goals of negotiating workplace conditions and terms of employment with their employer that we call collective bargaining ... Acts of bad faith, or unilateral nullification of negotiated terms, without any process of meaningful discussion and consultation may also significantly undermine the process of collective bargaining. (*B.C. Health Services* 2007: para. 91 and 92)

The Court found that clauses in the legislation that prohibited bargaining over issues that had once been negotiable violated Section 2(d), whereas clauses which narrowed the definition of a successor employer, and hence denied some workers their rights to bargain, did not.

To say that the proffered protection of union rights was limited is generous.[3] Only government measures that seriously undermined the ability of workers to voice their concerns regarding workplace issues constituted potential violations of Section 2(d). So long as governments offer unions an opportunity to consult before acting, however, there is no violation. And even where, in such cases, governments fail to consult, there may still be no violation as it "may be justified under s. 1 of the *Charter*, as reasonable limits demonstrably justified in a free and democratic society" (*B.C. Health Services* 2007: para. 108).

Those who thought the Supreme Court's 2007 *B.C. Health Services* ruling went further than this were dismayed by the Court's subsequent 2011 ruling in the *Fraser* case.[4] This case concerned the constitutional validity of Ontario's *Agricultural Employees Protection Act* (AEPA), passed in the wake of the *Dunmore* ruling in an effort to comply with that decision without actually extending collective bargaining rights to agricultural workers. The United Food and Commercial Workers (UFCW) challenged the constitutionality of the AEPA on the grounds that it did not provide the same collective bargaining rights as the *Ontario Labour Relations Act*, but the Court denied the appeal. The Court's insistence in *Fraser* that it was simply following the reasoning of *B.C. Health Services* fully accords with our more restrictive interpretation, which is powerfully reinforced when the justices say that

> Good faith negotiation under s. 2(d) requires the parties to meet and engage in meaningful dialogue; it does not impose a particular process; it does not require the parties to conclude an agreement or accept any particular terms; it does not guarantee a legislated dispute resolution mechanism in the case of an impasse; and it protects only the right to a general process of collective bargaining, not to a particular model of labour relations, nor to a specific bargaining method. (*Ontario [Attorney General] v. Fraser* 2011: 6)

The Court's ruling in *Fraser* was that the Court of Appeal had overstated the right to collective bargaining under the Charter's section 2(d). This was "not an affirmation of a particular type of collective bargaining, such as the Wagner model which is dominant in Canada." As far as the Court was concerned, "the right to associate to achieve collective goals" would be met so long as the right of employees' associations to make representations to their employers was established in legislation, including via provisions "that the employer shall listen to oral representations, and read written representations, and acknowledge having read them." This was sufficient to establish "that the employer consider employee representations in good faith" (ibid.: 7–8).

When taken together with its decision in *Plourde v. Walmart* 2009 that the Charter's protection of freedom of association did not apply to the private sector, there is powerful evidence that the Supreme Court has effectively continued to underwrite the consolidation of permanent exceptionalism in the new millennium. This would prove very important in face of the way governments responded to the 2007–08 U.S. financial crisis and the rapidity with which it turned into the first great economic crisis of the twenty-first century.

THE CURRENT CRISIS AND LABOUR RIGHTS

The source of the current global economic crisis did not lie, as did the crisis of the 1970s, in the cauldron of inflation, declining profits or government fiscal deficits. It lay in the volatility of a finance order on which integrated transnational production and trade as well as consumer demand had become increasingly dependent. In this context, the seriousness of this crisis was not lost on the major capitalist states. As expressed at their first-ever summit in Washington, D.C., in 2008, and reiterated at the 2010 Toronto Summit amidst the infamous police assault on protestors, G20 leaders were above all concerned to reassure the banks and multinational corporations of their support for global capitalism by renewing their "commitment to refrain from raising barriers, or imposing new barriers to investment or trade in goods and services [and] minimize any negative impact on trade and investment of our domestic policy actions, including fiscal policy and action to support the financial sector" (quoted in Panitch and Gindin 2012: 333).

In terms of domestic policies, apart from massive bailouts of the banks and key industrial corporations in 2009, leaders of advanced capitalist countries undertook a coordinated fiscal intervention in a desperate bid to stave off economic collapse. Aided by the failure of the labour movement and the left generally to meaningfully intervene, governments managed to provide a certain economic stability. Then, beginning in 2010, governments turned to further consolidate the global neoliberal order, not least through embracing the need for public sector austerity (Albo, Gindin and Panitch 2010; Panitch and Gindin 2012).

Several factors account for this turn. One was the desire to align public sector wages and benefits with the new lower standard in the private sector, where the crisis had enabled companies to extract substantial concessions from their unionized workforces. No less important was the continuing power of the bond markets. Having bailed out the financial institutions that dominate these markets, governments had to assuage the financiers' orthodox concerns regarding inflation and that they would be repaid in a world of lower growth rates and stagnating government revenues.

In Canada, part and parcel of this was a further assault on workers' rights, with the federal government once again taking the lead. An early sign of this was the government's *Budget Implementation Act* of 2009, which included legislation removing the right of public sector workers to collectively pursue pay equity complaints at the Canadian Human Rights Commission and over-riding some negotiated salary increases. This was followed by several pieces of especially harsh back-to-work legislation in 2011–12 against workers at CP Rail, Air Canada and Canada Post respectively.

A central issue in the latter two cases was the companies' push for a two-tiered workplace (Bronskill 2011; Fudge 2011; Kennedy and Bouzane

2011; Cotroneo 2011; Deveau 2012; Stevens and Nesbitt 2012). Canada Post insisted on an inferior, defined contribution pension plan for its future employees, whereas Air Canada demanded a similarly inferior pension plan as well as lower wages and benefits for employees of its planned low-cost spinoff. The back-to-work legislation, requiring the arbitrator to choose the final offer of either the employer or the union, was clearly written to favour the employers. In the case of the postal workers, in addition to imposing a wage settlement that was less than Canada Post's last offer, the arbitrator was to be guided by the need for Canada Post to have "the necessary degree of flexibility to ensure its long term viability" and to ensure the "sustain-ability of its pension plan." The arbitrator was also required to take into account Canada Post's need to have "terms and conditions of employment that are consistent with those in comparable postal industries." Of course, most of the comparable industries have much lower rates of union density (Doorey 2012).

The federal government's assault was echoed in several provinces. In PEI, the government declared the employees of ambulance services essential workers, removing their right to strike in January 2011. A month later, the Québec government legislated an end to a two-week strike by government lawyers. In B.C., teachers were legislated back to work in March 2012 after being on strike for just three days, with the legislation requiring the arbitra-tor to impose an agreement adhering to the government's requirement for a "net zero" increase in education spending.[5]

But nowhere was the echo louder than in Ontario. The McGuinty Liberal government had long been remarkably sensitive to the concerns of the cor-porate sector generally and the bond markets specifically. As early as March 2009, concerns about the provincial deficit led McGuinty to threaten to cancel a planned increase in the minimum wage. By the fall of that year he was musing aloud about unpaid days off for provincial employees (Benzie 2009a, 2009b). This, however, did not dissuade the government from introducing a set of corporate tax cuts, which would see rates fall below the average for both the Great Lakes States and the OECD when fully implemented (Ontario Ministry of Finance 2009). Yet, apart from passing Bill 150, eliminating the right to strike for Toronto Transit workers in March 2011, the government was hesitant to act against the labour movement, sections of which had provided McGuinty with substantial support in previous elections. But the Supreme Court's 2007 *B.C. Health Services* ruling was also a factor, insofar as the government was concerned that it not fall afoul of the courts.

The Liberals next turned to the province's teachers' unions, which had proven reliable electoral allies since 1999 (Savage 2010). After achieving a deal with the unions representing teachers at the French language and separate school boards, the Liberals went after the holdouts with Bill 115 in September 2012, creating a two-year restraint period during which all collective agreements covering teachers were to contain a set of required terms, including a two-year wage freeze, three unpaid professional development days, a three-month delay in the payment of annual increments and a 50 percent cut to paid sick days. While the Bill did not explicitly remove the right to strike, it effectively did so by empowering Cabinet to impose local agreements with these terms where they were not reached "voluntarily" by December 3, 2012, and earlier if the minister believed an agreement would not be reached by that date. It also included a clause that exempted the bill from being challenged in the courts.

The McGuinty government then moved on to the rest of the public sector and, as with the teachers, went to great lengths to appear to be consulting with the unions. In the background, it was preparing legislation broad enough to allow "the responsible Minister to veto a collective agreement, override any collective agreement provision ... and impose any collective agreement provision" right across the public sector for as long as the provincial budget remained in deficit (Sack Goldblatt Mitchell 2012; Walkom 2012). Cynically named the *Protecting Public Services Act*, the proposed legislation was forestalled by McGuinty's sudden resignation as leader of the Liberal Party in October 2012. Hints were circulated in the press that the simultaneous prorogation of the legislature until a new leader was elected was intended to facilitate consultations with the unions to secure a "voluntary" wage freeze rather than have to rely on such blatantly coercive legislation. Perhaps — but another possible explanation for prorogation, also mooted in the press, was that the Liberals wanted to avoid being excoriated in the legislature for having paid out $149 million in compensation to eight hedge funds registered in the U.S. and the Cayman Islands. These hedge funds had agreed to provide financing to the firm contracted by the Ontario government to construct a power plant in West Toronto, a project the government subsequently cancelled in the face of local opposition. Although the firm had borrowed only $61 million from the hedge funds by the time the project was cancelled, they sued the government for $300 million in damages. Anticipating the damage to Ontario's reputation in international financial markets should the case go forward, the government agreed to pay the $61 million to the hedge funds plus $88 million in damages, yielding them a return just under the 60 percent limit on usury allowed under the Canadian Criminal Code (Howlett and Waldie 2012). This graphically expressed the grotesque asymmetry between the way financial capital and labour unions were treated throughout the era of neoliberal globalization.

CONCLUSION

The assault on labour rights that developed in the wake of the economic crisis of the mid 1970s was not a temporary phenomenon but a permanent shift toward greater reliance on coercion to subordinate workers to the exigencies of sustained capital accumulation that has continued through the 2007 financial crisis and up to the present. The labour movement certainly has not simply acquiesced to this assault. But insofar as it can be said to have had a strategy, appealing to the courts has been central to it.

If this strategy was somewhat decentred by the Supreme Court's 1987 *Trilogy* ruling, it returned to centre stage with the Supreme Court's 2007 *B.C. Health Services* ruling. Expectations that this decision might draw a firm line against the continued use of coercive legislation against basic union rights and freedoms should already have been dashed by the subsequent extensive resort to just such laws, led by the federal government. While the Court's interpretation of freedom of association is far from settled, it would be naive for the labour movement to rely on the courts. To limit union strategy to the judicial arena is to ignore the extent to which court decisions are shaped by broader economic and political forces (Fudge 2008; Savage 2009; Smith 2012).[6] Workers would not have secured collective rights in the first place without fighting "in the streets." At the same time, no union can defy the law on its own; the support of others is necessary. However, the labour movement is marked by a pervasive sectionalism, with solidarity overwhelmingly built around specific demands in a given workplace (Swartz and Warskett 2012). This did not preclude unionized workers from making gains in the past or even from enjoying the support of other workers who could envision these gains spreading to them. But today, unionized workers who have reasonable wages or benefits are often objects of resentment, which makes defending past gains more difficult. As Sam Gindin (2012: 28–29) has noted, "limited in their vision and fragmented in their structures, unions have been no match for the offensives of employers and, above all, those of the state."

The task of building a broader solidarity will involve articulating common class interests capable of mobilizing broad popular support. To be sure, part and parcel of any struggle to defend workers' collective rights is developing a discourse that ties these rights to expanding the meaning of freedom of association. Yet even in this regard, the grounds for hope lie less in anticipated court rulings than in the successful 2012 Québec student strike and what it has demonstrated in terms of building popular support. And just as public sector unions have borne the brunt of the assault on union freedoms, so does it fall to them to take the lead in developing new collective capacities to struggle that integrate the defence and indeed enhancement of public services with the deepening of democratic rights and freedoms.

Notes

1. The 1982 wage freeze was not the first such intervention: the Trudeau Liberals had earlier introduced the 1975–78 statutory wage and price controls.
2. The Hospital Employees' Union (HEU) initially engaged in a range of protest activities and indeed called for a Day of Protest involving a one-day work stoppage. For a number of reasons, including the declaration by the B.C. Labour Board that it would be an illegal strike, the protests were halted (Camfield 2006).
3. This assumes that the criteria for "meaningful" and "good faith" aren't exacting. For a thoughtful discussion, see Fudge (2008), who reaches a broadly similar conclusion to ours.
4. See, for example, Fudge 2011. Based on his lengthy opinion in *Ontario (Attorney General) v. Fraser* attacking the decision in *B.C. Health Services*, Justice Rothstein held a similar view of it although it was one he hardly welcomed.
5. The bill contained a number of other regressive changes that were set aside when the teachers reached an agreement with the government (Annis 2012).
6. A complementary argument can be found in Fudge 2008: 46–47.

3. PUBLIC SECTOR UNIONS AND ELECTORAL POLITICS IN CANADA

Larry Savage and Charles W. Smith

In the realm of electoral politics, Canada's public sector unions are incredibly fragmented. These divisions manifest themselves both regionally and ideologically. For example, provincial government employee unions in Manitoba, Saskatchewan and British Columbia steadfastly support provincial sections of the New Democratic Party (NDP), whereas electoral pacts between teachers' unions and the Ontario Liberal Party were a defining feature of the province's political scene throughout the 2000s. In Québec, there have long existed pockets of public sector union support for sovereignist parties, while in Ontario, the Provincial Police Association's endorsement of the Progressive Conservatives in the 1999 provincial election (CBC News 1999) made evident the diversity of partisan allegiances that exist among public sector unions in Canada. Equally diverse are the electoral tactics used by public sector unions to influence election outcomes. From the politics of strategic voting, to electoral abstinence, to fierce electoral loyalty to a single party, to the instrumental strategy of "rewarding your friends and punishing your enemies," public sector unions participate in a range of different electoral activities, sometimes at cross purposes (Savage 2012).

This chapter is concerned with the relationship between public sector unions and electoral politics in Canada. We begin with a brief history of public sector political struggles with a view to demonstrating that both the nature and structure of public sector work discouraged, or legally restricted, public sector workers and their unions from engaging in electoral activities well into the postwar era. We then turn to the creation and growth of the NDP and explore why some public sector unions gravitated toward the social democratic party, while others maintained nonpartisan political stances or sought partisan links with different political parties in different regions of the country. We follow up with a discussion concerning the uncomfortable dual role that social democratic governments play as both allies and employers of public sector workers, focusing on the functions and limitations of forming government in advanced capitalist democracies. Finally, we share some concluding thoughts on the future of public sector unions and electoral politics, arguing that an exclusive focus on parties and elections cannot solve the structural problems that confront public sector unions and their members in an era of neoliberal restructuring.

A BRIEF HISTORY OF PUBLIC SECTOR UNIONS AND ELECTORAL POLITICS

Throughout much of Canada's history, the law forbade or severely restricted federal and provincial government employees from engaging in independent political action. These restrictions on political freedoms reflected the prevailing attitude of political elites, who viewed public sector workers as servants of the government rather than workers with full economic and political rights. Admittedly, most public sector workers in these early years were not overtly political, nor were they demanding full rights to unionization (Roberts 1994: 12–15). However, by the 1960s, the political, economic and cultural landscape began to radically shift (Palmer 2009). The expansion of Canada's postwar welfare state alongside the hierarchical, paternalistic and authoritarian structures that governed Canada's civil service eroded many of the historical ties that bonded public sector workers with government. In many cases, these struggles were exacerbated by changes within the workplace, which saw modern "private-sector management practices ... put in place to impose capitalist practices of efficiency on public workers" (Heron 2012: 95).

These structural changes in the public sector workplace coincided with a radical demographic shift among public sector workers. In the 1960s and 1970s, the public sector across the country became increasingly diverse, with more women and workers from different linguistic, ethnic and class positions delivering services to a changing Canadian society (Sangster 2010: 20–22). Many of these workers, maligned by discriminatory management practices, looked to unionization and political action as ways of improving the quality and security of public sector work.

In the late 1960s, the federal government (and later the provinces) finally acceded to demands for reform by making changes to how the civil service was governed. In 1967, the federal government passed the *Public Service Employment Act*, which extended more concrete rights of public sector workers to participate (as private citizens) in the electoral process. In that same year, the Liberal minority government, under pressure from the NDP, also passed the *Public Service Staff Relations Act (PSSRA)*, which extended certification rights to most public sector workers in the federal public service. According to close observers of the federal public service, these developments "marked the first step away from the belief that a politically neutral public service requires the denial of most political rights to all public servants and toward the understanding that political inactivity by all public servants is not necessarily prerequisite to their efficiency and loyalty" (Dwivedi and Gow 1999: 73). The changes to the federal public service in this period marked a real transition in the nature of public sector work. Although similar changes were slow to take root in many of the provinces (Ontario, Alberta, PEI and Nova Scotia all made public sector strikes illegal), the PSSRA changed the face of the Canadian labour movement (Panitch and Swartz 2003: 19). By the end of the 1970s, public sector unions had more members than their private sector counterparts (Palmer 1992: 353–4).

With few exceptions, public sector unions formed during this period tended to be organized in the fashion dictated by the *Public Service Employment Act* (ibid.: 354–5; Panitch and Swartz 2003: 21). The relative absence of internal militancy in the formation of these unions weakened their potential political capacity to transform the hierarchical and bureaucratic nature of the public sector workplace. As a result, many public sector unions were unprepared to challenge governments when the public sector collective bargaining framework was rewritten in the 1970s and 1980s in ways that allowed governments to permanently run roughshod over union rights to strike and bargain collectively (Panitch and Swartz 2003).

TESTING THE WATERS:
PUBLIC SECTOR UNIONS AND ELECTORAL POLITICS, 1960–1990

Given the dominant nonpartisan orientation of public sector unions in the immediate postwar period and given the restrictions on the rights of some public sector workers to engage in political activities, very few public sector unions were actively involved in electoral politics prior to the passage of the PSSRA (or the equivalent in the provinces). It is not surprising, then, that only one of the 573 officially registered labour delegates at the NDP's founding convention represented a public sector union.[1] The lack of public sector union involvement in the formation of the party confirmed the relatively insignificant role that these unions played in the development of the NDP (Horowitz 1968: 233). In fact, some public sector unions actively opposed the creation of the new party. The Alberta Civil Servants' Association, the Newfoundland Government Employees' Association and the National Unemployment Insurance Commission Employees' Association all disaffiliated from the Canadian Labour Congress (CLC) over the latter's decision to launch the NDP, citing the need to preserve impartial relations with government (ibid.: 243–4). Similarly, the Hamilton Municipal Employees' Association quit the Ontario Federation of Labour (OFL) over the latter's support for the NDP because, as President Herb Barker explained, "on city council we have to deal with people in all parties. We have found good friends among Liberals and Conservatives. They have never let politics interfere with their dealings with us and we feel we should do the same" (quoted in Horowitz 1968: 244). At the 1961 convention of the National Union of Public Employees (NUPE), President William Buss, in his opening address, lamented:

> in my opinion, since the decision of Congress to join with the Canadian [sic] Commonwealth Federation to form the New Party, a great deal of restrictive legislation has emanated from the various levels of government towards trade unions, which affects the affiliates of our National Union. It is also my opinion, while there is no actual proof that the National Union has suffered within the Trade Union Movement because of its decision not to take part in political action, I am sure this is known among the various divisions, district councils and local unions. (NUPE 1961: 10)

This early nonpartisan mentality suggests that many public sector union leaders continued to maintain an idealistic image of their members as "public servants" rather than workers whose interests stood in opposition to those of their employers. It was this traditional notion of the public worker as a "servant" that no doubt influenced Keith Archer's decision to exclude public sector unions from his study of the NDP-labour relationship. Archer adopted this position based on the rather peculiar normative claim that

> insofar as union affiliation is concerned, government is the employer for public sector unionists. Because it is the employer, and because there is a strong potential for them to have adversarial roles in the collective bargaining process, it is not appropriate for these unions to affiliate themselves with any party, including the NDP. (Archer 1990: 44)

The fact is, however, before Archer's book was even published, public sector unionists had long constituted a majority of all union members in Canada, and some important public sector unions, like the Canadian Union of Public Employees (CUPE), shared close ties to the party, particularly at the leadership level. In 1965, the national CUPE convention adopted a somewhat cautious resolution "to take positive action in support of the New Democratic Party, compatible with the autonomy of individual local unions" (CUPE 1985: 29) but followed up in 1967 with a resolution calling for the union to "institute a more extensive program to educate the membership on the platform of the New Democratic Party, and how it affects them personally, to promote greater interest in politics and local union affiliation to the NDP" (ibid.).

On one level, increasing public sector union support for the NDP was perfectly rational given that public sector workers, by virtue of their employment relationship, had the most to gain — and to lose — from direct involvement in electoral politics. Some public sector unions, in effect, saw elections as an opportunity to choose the "best" public sector managers who could be trusted to govern in labour's interest. For example, in a report to the 1973 CUPE national convention, the director of the union's Prairie region reported that, in Saskatchewan, the change from the

> oppression of the [Liberal] Thatcher government to the pro-labour positions of the Blakeney [NDP] government on many questions is felt by almost all our members. They are aware of the need for political action and do not believe that public employees can afford to appear politically neutral. (CUPE 1973: 69)

Despite increased public sector union interest in the NDP throughout the 1970s and 1980s, the party continued to be dominated by numerically smaller private sector unions (Archer 1990; Archer and Whitehorn 1997). In fact, with the exception of isolated regional pockets in places like Manitoba, public sector unions have never enjoyed strong influence within the party. The comparative weakness of the public sector union–NDP relationship was due to several factors. First, support for the NDP was highly contentious within public sector unions themselves, largely because many workers felt caught between their role as servants of the public — which implies a tacit, if not outright, support for their employers — and demands for greater workplace rights and better terms and conditions of employment. Second, the decentralized nature of the NDP's affiliation structure discouraged the growth of formal institutional relationships with labour unions, particularly with highly decentralized unions like CUPE, because it left the question of affiliation to individual (and in some cases autonomous) union locals, whose political priorities were not always in line with the will of the national union (Ross 2005). Finally, draconian legislation limiting the political rights of federal and provincial government employees throughout the 1970s and 1980s discouraged official party-union ties (Cassidy 1986).[2]

However, the ascendency of neoliberalism in Canada served to push even the most reluctant public sector unions into the electoral arena, if not into the arms of the NDP. Progressive Conservative leader Brian Mulroney's 1984 campaign commitment to hand out "pink slips and running shoes to bureaucrats" (quoted in Zussman 1986: 255) understandably put federal government employees on edge but also reinforced the need for all public sector workers to engage in political action in defence of their own employment interests.

During the 1980s, individual members of the public service who were fighting for increased political rights (with the support of public service unions) went to court in order to challenge federal and provincial restrictions on political activity. In *Ontario Public Service Employees Union v. Ontario* (1986), the union argued that it was outside the jurisdiction of the provinces to restrict public sector workers from fundraising for federal political parties, expressing political opinions in public or running for office without being forced to take a leave. Ultimately, the union was unsuccessful in challenging the broad restrictions put in place by the Ontario government. Several years later, however, a group of federal public service workers and their unions successfully challenged similar restrictions to their political rights in the Supreme Court of Canada, arguing in *Osborne v. Canada* (1991) that such restrictions violated the guarantee of freedom of expression in the Charter of Rights and Freedoms (*Osborne v. Canada [Treasury Board]* 1991).

After the *Osborne* decision, a growing number of public sector unions began intervening in electoral politics in more overtly partisan ways. Whereas most government employee unions had fought for political rights on the somewhat limited basis that public sector union members ought to have the unfettered right to volunteer for a candidate or display a lawn sign, some public service unions gradually seized upon the opportunity to exercise their political rights in more collective and organized ways. For example, the Public Service Alliance of Canada began endorsing NDP, Liberal and Bloc Québécois (BQ) candidates in and around the National Capital Region beginning in 2006, and the Ontario Public Service Employees Union joined the province's teachers' unions in endorsing select New Democrats and Liberals beginning in the 1999 provincial election, all in an effort to prevent anti-union Conservative parties from winning power (Savage 2010).

The diversity of electoral approaches among public sector unions makes it difficult to employ one particular model for understanding public sector union–political party relationships. While Jansen and Young (2009) have argued that ideological affinity, rather than rational self-interest, best explains the enduring relationship between the NDP and Canada's labour movement, their analysis does not distinguish between private sector and public sector unions and fails to take into consideration important regional differences. In contrast, following Pilon, Ross and Savage (2011), we maintain that public sector union–political party relationships are generally influenced by several political-economic factors, including a union's structural location vis-à-vis the state, its political culture and the political priorities of its leaders. In addition to paying particular attention to issues of locality and culture, understanding the historical linkages between the union, the state and the broader working class are essential. In the words of Pilon, Ross and Savage (2011: 33),

> history and politics matter; the labour movement's political practices are the result of lessons learned in the attempts to cope, respond to and resist changes in political economic structures and processes. They are not determined by them in a simple way; nor will legislative change strip away the accumulation of political experience.

This more nuanced view of party-union relationships helps us to better understand the enduring partisan ties between some segments of the labour movement and Canada's social democratic party, even when that relationship has become strained when the NDP has formed government.

PUBLIC SECTOR UNIONS, SOCIAL DEMOCRACY AND ELECTORAL POLITICS IN THE NEOLIBERAL ERA, 1990–2013

Social democratic governments have long struggled with their dual responsibility as a political ally of organized labour on one hand and as a public sector employer on the other. Whereas social democratic parties have been known to act as a "voice of labour" while in opposition, they have also been known to emphasize their role as the "voice of the employer" once they transition to government. As such, public sector unions have always maintained a contradictory relationship with political parties loosely aligned with the organized labor movement, due largely to government's management of the public purse.

In Canada, successive NDP provincial governments reinforced this tension through a series of neoliberal provincial austerity programs in the 1990s that often limited the capacity of public sector workers to organize, bargain and strike (McBride 2005). In Ontario, the NDP government's decision to address the province's growing debt and deficit by adopting a "Social Contract" — a fiscal austerity program that rolled back wages and suspended collective bargaining rights in the public sector — was met with fierce opposition and resistance by public sector unions and had negative repercussions for union–party relations across the country in the early 1990s (Panitch and Swartz 2003: 172–81; Hargrove 2009: 120). The party's attack on free collective bargaining in the public sector prompted a massive revolt from the labour movement. A number of union locals disaffiliated from the party, CUPE's Julie Davis resigned as President of the Ontario NDP in protest (Walkom 1994: 122) and the vast majority of public sector unions stopped donating money and other resources to the party. The Rae government was soundly defeated in 1995, only to be replaced by the militantly anti-union Mike Harris Conservative government. The Ontario Tories wasted no time rolling back workers' rights as part of a wider strategy to weaken the labour movement. In the years that followed, some of the public sector unions targeted by the NDP's Social Contract (unions of teachers and nurses most notably) drifted into a strategic alliance with the more electorally viable Ontario Liberal Party, in part to shield themselves from the worst aspects of the Conservative Party's anti-labour agenda (Savage 2010). This strategy also reflected openness among public sector unions to engage in quid pro quo relationships with parties of varying political stripes.

In the Prairie provinces, the NDP's relationship with public sector unions has also sometimes been stormy. In 1982, on the eve of a Saskatchewan provincial election, NDP premier Alan Blakeney used back-to-work legislation to end a legal CUPE strike in the province's hospitals (Smith 2011: 125–8). The move alienated many in the labour movement and contributed to the government's eventual defeat. The situation was further exacerbated a decade later when Roy Romanow became premier. Throughout his premiership, Romanow maintained a tense relationship with the province's labour unions (Smith 2011). When Romanow used back-to-work legislation to end strikes by nurses and power utility workers in the late 1990s, he further reinforced that tension (Smith 2011: 135–6). In private, the union leadership was livid that the party interfered with workers' right to strike, but in public, most labour leaders were careful not to criticize the party's intervention (Byers 2002: 75). According to John Warnock (2004: 95), "with labour in its back pocket, the NDP leadership has concluded that it has to do very little to retain labour's support." Manitoba's public sector unions have a similar relationship to the party. In that province, many public sector unions have seemingly taken the position that the NDP, despite its increasingly neoliberal character, must be supported to prevent the ascendance of an even more right-wing party (Savage 2010: 18).

In British Columbia, the NDP government's record on labour issues in the 1990s was mixed (Carroll and Ratner 2005; Stanford 2001). While the government did initiate a ban on the use of replacement workers, it also fiercely promoted public sector austerity as a way to combat budget deficits. In relation to NDP governments in all Western provinces, Bryan Evans (2012: 59) has noted: "In provinces where the NDP faces a single right-wing competitor, organized labour fears the right-wing party more than the NDP's fair-weather friendship."

The dynamic of the NDP–public sector union relationship in English Canada is not dissimilar to the relationship between the Parti Quebecois (PQ) and public sector unions in Québec. Although not a traditional labour party, the sovereignist PQ does tend to share closer relations with unions than do other parties in Québec. The Québec Federation of Labour (QFL), the largest union central in the province, is viewed as having the most intimate relationship with the PQ, having officially endorsed the party in five of the last ten provincial elections.[3] The QFL has also periodically endorsed the PQ's federal cousin, the Bloc Quebecois, in federal elections (Savage 2010: 22–23). While other Québec labour organizations, specifically the Confédération des syndicats nationaux (CSN) and the Centrale des syndicats du Québec (CSQ) — which have a greater proportion of members working in the public sector — have often found themselves at odds with PQ governments, many from within their ranks have played prominent roles in the party. The Québec labour movement's support for sovereignty has played a key role in sustaining its generally warm relationship with the PQ (Graefe 2005; Savage 2008b). However, this relationship is not without contradictions. After the PQ government embraced public sector austerity programs in the early 1980s and late 1990s respectively, their union allies withdrew support. The Conseil central du Montréal métropolitain CSN (CCMM) explained organized labour's dilemma in prioritizing its politics under a PQ government as follows:

> Let's be clear, we have sometimes had difficulty developing and articulating our strategies when the Québec state is governed by sovereignists. Our positions on the national question and the importance that we attach to it for resolving the social question, from time to time, pose strategic problems. Of course, far be it from us to question our position on Québec sovereignty. However, we believe there is a real problem in our ranks when the PQ is in power. Not in words, but in practice. (Conseil central du Montréal métropolitain, n.d.)[4]

THE FUTURE OF PUBLIC SECTOR UNIONS AND ELECTORAL POLITICS

In an era of neoliberal austerity, public sector unions cannot afford to remain politically neutral, especially when they risk losing at the ballot box what they gain at the bargaining table. The real question for public sector unions is what method of electoral intervention makes the most strategic sense. While public sector union endorsements of Liberal or Conservative candidates come with obvious risks, so too does an exclusive electoral alliance with the NDP. In the face of unprecedented neoliberal austerity, providing automatic and unconditional support to a social democratic political party in the hope that it will defend the rights of public sector workers is a dubious strategy. If, as Bryan Evans (2012: 59) argues, "the neoliberal shift apparent in every provincial NDP government elected since 1990 suggests that organized labour, and by extension the working class, have gained little from the NDP in government save perhaps being spared a more aggressive right-wing assault," it is clear that public sector unions need to tread carefully as far as traditional social democratic party–union relationships are concerned. The NDP's track record in government, consistent with the actions of social democratic parties in all advanced capitalist countries, demonstrates that neoliberalism has effectively repositioned even pro-labour parties to work in opposition to the labour movement (Seifert and Sibley 2011). This problem is compounded by the fact that the state itself remains a capitalist state, whether it is managed by social democrats or not. In this sense, public sector unions must confront the very real contradictions and limitations associated with electoral politics because they pose a real quandary for elements of the public sector labour movement that have a real interest in promoting and fighting for broader and more radical forms of social transformation.

This is not meant to imply that public sector unions should abandon the electoral realm altogether. While it is true that fighting to manage the capitalist state still means managing a capitalist state, even under the conditions of neoliberalism, the question of who governs is still important. That said, public sector workers must recognize that support for nominally pro-union parties can only offer short-term solutions at best if those parties are not under significant and sustained pressure from workers' movements and their allies. In the words of Hurley and Gindin (2011), unions cannot allow "electoral activity to replace the independent mobilizations of the trade union movement." No government, social democratic or otherwise, will openly concede its power over the workplace, the public purse or its perceived monopoly over what constitutes the public interest. As a result, public sector unions must recognize that the election of a political ally is only the beginning of the struggle for social change. In short, what really matters is what public sector unions do beyond the ballot box, in between election cycles, to influence state actors, mobilize members and build coalitions with like-minded social movements and workers' organizations, all with a view to challenging the bureaucratic, authoritarian structures that govern modern public service work and, in turn, demonstrating that public sector workers are vital to building a more progressive and egalitarian society.

Notes

1. The delegate was representing the National Union of Public Sector Employees, which later merged with the National Union of Public Employees to create the Canadian Union of Public Employees in 1963 (Horowitz 1968: 100).

2. Despite the relative lack of formal institutional linkages between public sector unions and the NDP, several high-profile public sector union leaders shared close ties to the party. Patrick Lenihan, one of the "founders of Canadian public service unionism," was active in launching and building the NDP in Alberta (Lenihan 1998: 196–8). CUPE's Shirley Carr, who later served as president of the CLC, ran as a candidate for the Ontario NDP. CUPE Ontario president, Sid Ryan, ran several times for the federal and provincial wings of the party in the Greater Toronto Area in the late 1990s and early to mid 2000s. CUPW President Jean Claude Parrot was an NDP supporter and encouraged his members to vote for the party (Parrot 2005: 283). PSAC president Nycole Turmel was elected as a New Democrat MP in Hull–Aylmer in 2011 and became interim leader of the party after the untimely death of Jack Layton. Some public sector union activists have even gone on to lead NDP governments. Former B.C. premier Dave Barrett was a member of the British Columbia Government Employees Union before entering politics, and former Manitoba premier Gary Doer served as president of the Manitoba Government Employees' Union before winning election to the provincial legislature.

3. Following the PQ's unprecedented attack on the rights of public sector workers in the early 1980s, the QFL withheld its endorsement in the 1985 provincial

election against the wishes of QFL President Louis Laberge. In 1989 and 1994 the QFL endorsed the PQ. In 1998 and 2003, the QFL declined to endorse the PQ, but did endorse the party in the 2007 provincial election. In 2008 and 2012, however, the QFL declined to endorse the PQ.

4. Translation by the authors.

4. SOCIAL UNIONISM AND UNION POWER IN PUBLIC SECTOR UNIONS

Stephanie Ross

Since the 1970s, the strategies of public sector unions in Canada have increasingly centred around social unionism, an orientation that entails a broader view of workers' interests (beyond the economic) and of the strategies necessary to achieve union goals (beyond the workplace and collective bargaining). Both the nature of public sector work and labour relations and the broader context of neoliberalism have made necessary messages and strategies that link public sector workers' interests with those of the public good. Despite important variations across and within unions, the public sector has become a vibrant terrain for a social unionist ethos and repertoire.

However, the adoption of social unionism as either a frame or strategy for public sector collective bargaining does not guarantee that public sector unions can effectively leverage greater union power to make or preserve economic gains. Indeed, many public sector unions' claims to represent the broader public interest have fallen on deaf ears, particularly in the context of the post-2008 wave of austerity measures. The concrete expressions of public sector social unionism vary widely as do their outcomes, not least because they take account of different sources of public sector union power. This chapter traces the major bases of the practice of social unionism in Canada's public sector unions and explores the contribution such strategies make to increasing public sector union power.

DEFINING SOCIAL UNIONISM

Like all union orientations or "modes of union praxis" (Camfield 2007: 284), social unionism involves a constellation of ideas about what unions do and why, whom they represent, what their interests are and how such interests are to be fought for and defended. Social unionism entails a collective action frame[1] that "legitimizes taking on broader community issues as the proper focus of union activity as well as strategies and tactics necessary to act effectively on those more broadly defined interests" (Hrynyshyn and Ross 2010: 9). The diagnosis of workers' problems rests on an (often implicit) analysis of class and other inequalities as pervading social relations rather than remaining contained — and hence solvable — within the workplace. Social unionists often invoke antisectionalist collective identities in that the community of solidarity is seen as broader than one's immediate workmates, occupation or industry. The terrain of struggle is also broader than the workplace, and the range of interests goes beyond wages and benefits, giving an anti-economist cast to social unionist messages. These two elements are often united in a vision of unionism as "the base from which broader social change is made in the interests of the working-class majority" rather than merely already-unionized workers (Ross 2012: 40). The resulting strategic repertoire thus extends beyond those processes linked to the postwar labour relations framework, which privileged, via legal and bureaucratic mechanisms, both the narrow workplace "community of interest" and the processes of collective bargaining and grievance arbitration as adequate solutions to workers' problems.

However, social unionism is also undoubtedly a contested term. Some commentators have opted to define it relatively narrowly, as a form of unionism with a somewhat broader social vision than business unionism, primarily wedded to nondisruptive political strategies of change and resting on still-bureaucratic relationships within labour organizations (Camfield this volume). While this does describe some variants of social unionism as practiced today, I have argued elsewhere (Ross 2007, 2008, 2012) that social unionism should be understood as a much broader category, with historically specific combinations of vision, strategy and organizational practices producing variations over time and across unions. For example, unions that adopt a social unionist framework will range in the militancy of their tactics, the radicalism of their goals and their commitment to internal democratic organization, all the while maintaining a broader vision of unions' proper role in society.

The Canadian labour movement has a long history of social unionist activism. The labour movement has either led or been prominent in the struggles for legislated labour reform (including health and safety legislation and prohibitions on child labour); to expand the social wage (including unemployment insurance, universal public health care, public education, public pensions, parental leave and universal child care); and to legislate pay and employment equity. Since the 1980s, the repertoires associated with social unionism have also become more prominent in many segments of the Canadian labour movement, which have entered into coalitions with other movements (Rapaport 1999: 58; Bleyer 1992; Panitch and Swartz 2003: 157).

Particular moments of heightened conflict have reinforced these tendencies. For instance, the 1988 federal election, which centred around the issue of free trade between Canada and the United States, forged a strong pole within the labour movement oriented to coalition-building with other progressive forces and knit together these allies with an ideological frame of the "corporate agenda," which served as an analysis of the source of problems and the larger issues at stake (Panitch and Swartz 2003: 158).

However, it is also clear that not all unions have embraced social unionism to the same extent. As Kumar and Murray (2002: 6) point out in their survey of union innovation, approximately 65 percent of unions indicate they are engaged in "political action to change public policy and bring about social and economic change," while 17.5 percent say they do not engage in such activity. Related to this finding is that 70 percent of their survey respondents were public sector union leaders, indicating a close relationship between such unions and a particular mode of union praxis (Kumar and Murray 2002: 4). This of course begs the question: why are public sector unions more likely than their private sector counterparts to adopt social unionist discourses and strategies?

SOURCES OF SOCIAL UNIONISM IN PUBLIC SECTOR UNIONS

The specificities of public sector unions have led them to adopt strategies increasingly centred around social unionism. First, as Paul Johnston (1994: 31) has argued, the satisfaction of public sector unions' economic interests is inherently tied to the outcome of policy debates that necessarily involve other citizens. Public sector unions have "a special relationship to the public agenda" because their sectional claims — for higher wages, more and secure jobs and improved working conditions — are inevitably bound up with contests about the "public good" and which public policies serve that good (ibid.). As a result, and in contrast to private sector unions, whose main strategy is to exert control over the labour market by regulating labour market entry and/or taking wages out of competition, public sector unions seek to "influence their terms of employment by creating alliances that represent a variety of interests — including, perhaps, those of other workers — across the political-bureaucratic division of labor" (Johnston 1994: 9). In that sense, public sector unions tend to be anti-economistic precisely because their power — and the power of their immediate opponent, the state or public agency as employer — is not primarily economic.

Second, the nature of many public sector jobs themselves brings public sector workers into regular contact with the broader community, thus forging particular types of occupational consciousness influenced by the content of public sector work. Public sector unionists' "self-understandings ... [tend] to be conditioned by their labour of service delivery" (Camfield 2005: 61).

Some workers, for example, are exposed to the challenges faced by service recipients, thus potentially promoting a sense of shared interest in the quality of public services. Case studies analyzing nurses (Coulter 1993), teachers (Camfield 2009), daycare workers (Kass and Costiglia 2004) and social service workers in the nonprofit sector (Baines 2010a) all document the framing of workers' own interests as part of a broader commitment to the conditions that allow for the provision of "proper service" to the public. The logic of feminized care work has fostered a specific occupational consciousness for public sector women, because the fulfillment of their work roles often creates a strong bond with those they serve. Public sector unions with a public safety mandate, such as those of firefighters or police officers, also mobilize notions of heroism and self-sacrifice for the sake of the public to buttress their sectional claims, often with great material success (Braedley 2009: 136–7). Similarly, while contradictory, professionalism can act as a source of social unionist ethos, because most professional codes include a responsibility to those who are served by the profession. Defending professional standards and autonomy often entails struggles for particular enabling working conditions, levels of funding and thus of service (Savage and Webber this volume). For Johnston (1994: 12), such an orientation pervades all public sector workers' thinking, because "for better or worse … they are involved in public issues: because they confront them face-to-face — at the point of production, so to speak, of society itself." Put another way, the material conditions of public sector workers' labour tends to encourage an occupational consciousness based on identification with the public.

Third, the fiscal crisis of the state and the subsequent rise of neoliberalism in the 1970s further reinforced the tendency toward social unionism. Cuts to public services and jobs twinned with restrictions on their collective bargaining rights through the practices of "permanent exceptionalism" (Panitch and Swartz this volume) — the latter often necessary to extract the desired concessions — have politicized public sector workers to varying extents. In fact, the Canadian state's actions have pushed many public sector unions into social unionism despite themselves. Many public sector unions originated with a desire to replicate the bureaucratized and professionalized forms of union power that became common in the postwar labour movement and were enforced by the legal industrial relations regime. CUPE's early leaders, for instance, saw professionalized collective bargaining as a key goal of the merger that formed the union in 1963 but were soon pushed to adopt more political strategies as they realized such professionalization would be insufficient (Ross 2005). Similar trajectories exist for teachers[2] (Laxer 1976; Hanson 2009), civil service associations[3] (Roberts 1994) and even engineers (Coulter 2009). Consistent government intervention in what was supposed to be "free collective bargaining" revealed the role and power of the state in public (and para-public) sector negotiations. It also revealed (albeit in partial and vague ways) the capitalist nature of the state as it weighed in on the side of employers, "labour discipline" and a "good business climate" (Langford 1994).

The limits placed on public sector collective bargaining have also led to a questioning of the legalism so embedded in the postwar labour relations regime, because it could not (or was not allowed to) deliver for public sector unions. These limits have had strategic implications for public sector unions. As Panitch and Swartz (2003: 156) argue,

> the realization that collective bargaining could not secure the same kinds of monetary wage gains as it did in the era of free collective bargaining and post-war boom, seemed to produce a capacity for workers' struggles around other issues that went well beyond just holding on to what had been gained before.

This is true in the labour movement in general, but also, quite specifically, in the public sector, having been subject to various legal restrictions on collective bargaining rights.[4] Through the 1970s and 80s,

> challenges to the ideology of legalism, which had been so immobilizing, were increasingly visible, evident in the growing frequency of strikes in outright defiance of laws that banned the right to strike … The turn toward coercion itself raised the right to strike to a matter of principle for many workers. Union strategies were, less and less, framed within the parameters of what the law permits. (Panitch and Swartz 2003: 156)

Such dynamics have made workplace-focused "pure and simple unionism" increasingly impossible for these unions, driven them to seek allies amongst the voting public and led them to engage in extraparliamentary mobilizations against neoliberalism (Camfield 2005: 57).

Fourth, we cannot overemphasize the particular role of union feminism in fuelling social unionist ideas and strategies in the Canadian labour movement in general and the public sector in particular. The public sector is the location for the vast majority of unionized women. In Canada, it has been well documented that union women's activism combined collective bargaining and political activism for a variety of reasons. Socialist feminists convincingly argued that women workers faced problems that straddled the public and private, work and home life, and thus required activism in multiple spaces (Luxton 2001). Women unionists also confronted male-dominated unions resistant to the broadening of the union agenda and who had the power to define that agenda (Briskin and McDermott 1993; see also Ross 2013).

This led union feminists to seek coalitions with feminists outside the labour movement and to fight for legislative solutions in addition to those derived from collective bargaining.

However, the concrete expressions of public sector social unionism vary widely, as do their outcomes. Social unionism has developed very unevenly in the public sector. Even though the basis of public sector work and labour relations is different from that in the private, on the whole it is still subject to the same industrial relations legal-institutional framework and its pressures on union action. As Donald Swartz and Rosemary Warskett (2012: 23) explain, postwar legislation establishing the legal basis for unions presented them

> with a whole new set of obstacles to expansive solidarity. By linking union recognition to state-defined bargaining units at specific workplaces, it channelled unions towards workplace bargaining and away from broadly based struggles, a constraint reinforced by the restrictions on sympathy strikes and secondary boycotts.

Public sector unions, particularly those in the para-public sector, are subject to the fragmenting effects of certification practices entrenched at labour boards and the resulting constraints on both strategic leverage and expansive notions of community and solidarity (Fudge 1993). Given their containment within these legal structures, the pressures to adopt traditional workplace-based strategies remain powerful, even for unions in the public sector.

Moreover, the public sector's anti-economism does not necessarily imply an antisectionalist orientation. In fact, definitions of the "public good" can be partial, can privilege some interests over others or can wrongly assume that the interests of workers and the public are always compatible. For instance, the intersection of professional discourses with social unionist ones is indeterminate. Some professionals' ability to work to professional standards can lead to advocacy for changes that directly benefit their clients, while others' desire to preserve their autonomy and their labour market power — rooted in their relative irreplaceability — can lead to the extraction of gains that come at the expense of service recipients, citizens or other legitimate social interests. As such, the "public" nature of the work does not always produce the same social unionist claims or outcomes.

This is also true because not all public sector workers have the same kind of contact with the public, which has both political-ideological and strategic implications. A more fine-grained theory of the state than is typical in labour relations helps us with this insight. Where state workers are positioned in different state apparatuses — of coercion or social order, of social reproduction or legitimation, of administration or of supporting capital accumulation — matters in terms of their relationship to both power holders and clients and hence shapes their consciousness and public expressions. We would never assume, for instance, that the unionism of police officers and nurses would take the same form, given that one is positioned in the coercive state apparatus while the other is one of the pillars of the postwar social wage.[5]

As a result, it is not a given that public sector workers are seen by either direct service recipients or the broader public as allies. Rather, depending on the form of interaction, the public can experience these workers as a barrier or obstacle to the things they need or want. The epithet "bureaucrat" speaks to this, and popular representations of bureaucratic irrationality or indifference at the Department of Motor Vehicles or the U.S. Postal Service depict this real (if overblown) tension. In the Canadian context, many public sector workers, such as case workers at Ontario Works, Employment Insurance or the Workplace Safety and Insurance Board, are made into vectors of neoliberal discipline at the point of production. The extent to which such workers accept these directives or resist them makes an enormous difference to whether attempts at coalition-building with the public are successful.[6] In other words, it is not just contact with the public at the point of production that matters but the manner of that contact, the way that public sector workers engage in that contact and the way that their unions attempt to intervene in those relationships.

Finally, as with social unionism in general, the gap between rhetoric and reality is crucial. As Benford and Snow (2000: 616, 620) argue, despite the common link between stated values and strategic actions, social movements can also be plagued by disjunctures between what is said and what is done. Michael Hurley and Sam Gindin (2010: 187) take up this point in their strategic assessment of what public sector unions need to do to respond to the attacks on their jobs and collective bargaining rights that have flowed from the Great Recession and the austerity measures that have followed.

> To argue we've always supported better social services, we must point to our progressive union conference resolutions and insist that the rich should be taxed to pay for decent services and that fair compensation is valid. But that won't convince those we need to reach. Our commitment must be proven in practice, through the priorities we set and carry out. This means making a strategic choice: we must reset our focus from traditional collective bargaining to the defence of public services as a primary priority and take on — in bargaining, in our relationships to service recipients and on the streets — the leadership of the fight for adequate, high-quality and responsive public services.

In other words, despite the strong tendencies toward social unionism, public sector unions are also subject to a whole series of countervailing pressures, which makes both analysis of their political expressions and strategic assessments of their actions more complex than is generally acknowledged. Moreover, these variations have major effects on the kinds of power that can and cannot be leveraged from "social unionist" ideas and strategies, particularly in the realm of collective bargaining.

PUBLIC SECTOR UNIONS, UNION POWER AND SOCIAL UNIONISM

This brings us to a key question: what is it about social unionist ideas and strategies that are understood to generate more power for public sector unions? While many unionists identify with social unionism for occupational, political and moral reasons, there must also be some practical advantage to this approach. This requires us to take stock of the various forms of power inherent in the labour-management relationship (not to mention the class relations between workers, capitalists and the state) and to understand how (differently situated) unions seek to deploy that power.

John Godard (2011: 14) lays out a range of power resources embedded in the employment relationship, which he terms "relational" forms of power and which either party may possess. From workers' vantage point, these include: job power, wherein the knowledge required in the labour process is embedded in and thus dependent on the worker, giving them the capacity to interfere with management prerogatives; strike power, a temporary exit from the labour process that imposes costs on management; and exit power, exercised when a worker's leaving the employment relationship permanently imposes greater cost on the employer. Workers' exit power is strongly related to their labour market power, the extent to which they are able to find other work because their labour is scarce and difficult to replace. We can add a fifth form of workers' power, that of voice, the capacity to mount criticisms and effectively advocate for changes in the relationship (Hirschman 1970).

In this context, unions are a specific way to collectivize workers' power at the workplace and to amplify their labour market, voice, job, strike and exit power. Many of the techniques for doing this are well known, including controlling labour market entry (via mandatory apprenticeships or profes-sional certification); collective bargaining, the grievance procedure and other mechanisms for protecting workers who complain; and job control union-ism, in which job content and movement around internal labour markets is controlled. Moreover, strike power is clearly a collective power for workers, for which unionization provides some legal protection (although it also im-poses many limits).

There is an assumption, however, that these forms of power are pri-marily located in the employment relationship. Lévesque and Murray's (2002) framework for understanding the bases of local union power helps us focus on forms of power that transcend (but impact) the labour-manage-ment relationship. For them, there are three main elements of local union power: 1) proactivity, the union's capacity "to shape and put forward their own agenda ... demands ... projects ... and vision of social relations," in other words, to frame and maintain an analysis independent from that of capital/the employer; 2) internal solidarity,[7] "the mechanisms developed in the workplace to ensure democracy and collective cohesion amongst workers"; and 3) external solidarity, "the capacity of ... unions to work with their communities ... to build horizontal and vertical coordination ... with other unions" and to construct "alliances among unions, community groups and social movements" (Lévesque and Murray 2002: 45–46). These factors have a strong impact on how successfully unions can deploy the forms of power discussed by Godard.

However, neither of these analyses explicitly confront the way these forms of power are not necessarily equally important or available to all unions for them to achieve their goals. Some workers/unions can be successful using different combinations of these sources of power (given their labour market positions, etc.). This is why accounting for the distinct sources of public sector unions' power is important. According to Johnston (1994: 11), public sector workers face "different strategic conditions" because their power is rooted in "political-organizational" rather than economic resources. Johnston (ibid.) enumerates these forms of power in this way:

> first, legal rights, organizational status, and established procedures; second, strategic alliances within the shifting political universe of the public agency, including clients, constituents and other participants in that political universe; third, forms of voice that can help mobilize new organizing, build or prevent alliances and, by framing and appealing to "the public interest," put a potent political edge on the workers' demands.

As I have argued above, in the Canadian context, given the repeated attack on the legal rights of public sector workers, the latter two strategies of alliance-building (external solidarity) and voice (proactive framing) have become even more crucial.

This is particularly true if we examine the conditions in which public sector workers' strike power becomes effective. It has been amply demonstrated by Briskin (2007a) that public sector workers' militancy has been significant and growing since the 1970s. One of Camfield's (2005: 61) criticisms of Johnston is precisely his lack of attention to some public sector unions' "most potent power resource":

> the ability to bring state activities to a halt by striking. For many public sector workers, this is a structural capacity which they possess whether or not they have the legal right to strike; its exercise not

only disrupts the provision of services but throws a wrench into the state's political administration of civil society.

However, while this is true in the abstract, the concrete capacity of such unions to have such disruption become a resource on their side is highly contingent. Because public sector strikes often "help" the employer by saving them the money they would otherwise spend on wages, they cannot be understood as a form of economic leverage as is the case in the private sector. Rather, a public sector strike is a form of indirect political power, in that its impact on decision-makers depends crucially on the union's capacity to mobilize third parties to act on their behalf and on their side, rather than on that of the employer.

The bystander public is crucial to social movement mobilization in general, but especially so in the case of public sector unions. Gamson (2008) explains how transforming bystanders into allies is a crucial strategic element, because "neutrality" is not actually neutral. In some contests, "large portions of the gallery" may be more motivated by "the incidental personal injury or inconvenience they may suffer from the continuation of conflict" than by identification with other pre-existing forms of identity or community they may be notionally part of. "The bystander's slogan is 'a plague on both your houses!'" because for them "the primary issue [is] restoration of order and elimination of danger and inconvenience" (Turner and Killan quoted in Gamson 2008: 244). Gamson (2008: 245) points out that "bystander frames render issue disagreements secondary to whatever policies will get the issue off the agenda" and that media often play an important role in mobilizing and highlighting this frame.

Given their unique position, public sector unions must take seriously the political-strategic impact of bystanders on both their labour relations and public policy struggles. This fact makes the mobilization of the various forms of union power, especially strike power, quite different from that in the private sector.[8] Although some public sector workers are more able to rely on their job and labour market power — that is, their relative irreplaceability — to amplify or substitute for strike power, many are not.[9] Thus, outcomes hang on whether public sector unions can develop and deploy their proactive capacity to frame conflicts and construct alliances in ways that mobilize both their own members and relevant segments of the public on their side. In other words social unionist frames and strategies are more important in public sector unions' calculations, even when acting on the terrain of collective bargaining.

However, there is caution to be exercised here. Not all social unionism is created equally. As I've argued elsewhere (Ross 2007, 2008), it is possible to adopt social unionist language and tactics without fostering a deep connection between the interests of workers and the public. Many unions make instrumental use of social unionism, which can foster cynicism when the immediate crisis these strategies are meant to address passes. Also, the extent to which social unionist efforts foster internal solidarity and democracy, as explored by Camfield (this volume), makes a real difference to their effectiveness, particularly as membership commitment is crucial to withstanding employer and state efforts to demonize worker militancy. Moreover, even at its best, social unionism is not a silver bullet. Given the preponderance of legal power on the part of the state (and indirectly, employers), even the most effective social unionist campaign can be overpowered by legislative interventions.

Ultimately, social unionism should not be seen merely as a set of tactics or just another way to extract gains for particular groups of workers from the labour relations framework, even though it does contribute to such gains. Instead, social unionism should be viewed as part of a long-term strategy of movement-building, in which each particular conflict is an opportunity to politicize collective bargaining, to make the connection between the interests of different segments of society — and of the working class in particular — and to develop the capacities for fighting for broader social transformation beyond the workplace.

Notes

1. Social movements' frames are political, ideological and cultural constructs that provide a particular explanation of the world so as "to mobilize potential adherents and constituents, to garner bystander support and to demobilize antagonists" (Snow and Benford 1988: 198).
2. Ontario teachers had engaged in prior waves of militancy, most notably in the 1973–75 mass resignations campaign to oppose the imposition of compulsory arbitration by the Davis Government (Laxer 1976: 217–24).
3. Similarly, the Ontario Public Service Employees Union (OPSEU), whose Ontario Public Service sector had just gained the right to strike in 1994 (Rapaport 1999: 28), was the first to face the Harris cuts in the context of collective bargaining, and their strike in 1995 rapidly politicized (not least because of the significant amount of violence involved in policing the strike) and became a lightning rod for broader opposition to the government. Ontario Federation of Labour president Gord Wilson characterized the OPSEU strike as "one of the first jets that lifted the rocket off" (Rapaport 1999: 56).
4. These restrictions have been extensively documented by Panitch and Swartz (2003 and this volume).
5. Johnston (1994: 15–16) makes this point in his discussion of various municipal workers, some of whom are articulated to progrowth coalitions led by local capitalists, while others are attached to social welfare, social consumption and dealing with the problems produced by capitalism.
6. See McElligott (2001) for a discussion of federal public sector workers organizing

to help clients resist restrictive EI policies.

7. The importance of internal solidarity and democracy to union power is explored in Camfield's chapter in this volume.

8. Recent developments at the federal level in Canada — and the federal government's willingness to intervene in private sector labour relations conflicts because they will disrupt "the fragile economy" — may be eroding this distinctiveness.

9. For instance, the professional workers discussed by Savage and Webber (this volume) report that collective bargaining in the past was characterized by managerial acceptance of (if not deference to) the workers' expertise and therefore of their legitimate claims to better wages and working conditions. As that acceptance has waned, eroding professionals' perceived job power, these unions have had to explore the forms of power that come from social unionist tactics.

5. RENEWING PUBLIC SECTOR UNIONS[1]

David Camfield

To have the best chance of defending themselves from the offensive against them, it is clear that public sector unionists need to do whatever they can to increase their power. This raises the idea of union renewal. This term has become common among university and union researchers concerned with the future of unions. It "is used to describe the process of change, underway or desired, to 'put new life and vigour' in the labour movement to rebuild its organizational and institutional strength" (Kumar and Schenk 2006: 30). This chapter argues that the best way to renew public sector unions is by radically changing what kind of unionism is practiced. The alternative approach advanced in this chapter is social movement unionism.

THREATS TO PUBLIC SECTOR UNIONS

All discussion of union renewal in public sector unions needs to start with a serious effort to understand the threats to unions that make renewal an urgent matter. The magnitude of these threats is not always fully appreciated, which is one reason why many union officers, staff and rank-and-file activists are not in practice treating change in public sector unions as urgent.

Perhaps the most obvious threat is blatant government attacks on the rights of public sector unions using legislation (Panitch and Swartz this volume). In a few cases, rights have simply been eliminated. For example, in 2011, Ontario's Bill 150 took away the right to strike from workers at the Toronto Transit Commission. As former Ontario Federation of Labour president Gord Wilson (2011) asked, "Who might be next?" More frequently, governments have, in the tradition of permanent exceptionalism (Panitch and Swartz this volume), temporarily suspended collective bargaining rights and prohibited bargaining on certain issues. Recent examples include British Columbia's Bill 22, directed against teachers (CBC News 2011a), and Ontario's Bill 115, which gave "absolute authority" to the "Minister of Education to unilaterally accept, reject or ultimately impose collective agreements upon Ontario education workers" (Cooke 2013).[2] Government attacks also include legislation to end or pre-emptively ban specific work stoppages, such as the federal legislation to end the 2011 dispute between the Canadian Union of Postal Workers (CUPW) and Canada Post Corporation (CPC) (Camfield 2011b).

More common than anti-union legislation is aggressive employer demands for concessions in collective bargaining. Public sector workers are experiencing declining real wages: pay increases in contracts covering five hundred or more workers averaged 1.7 percent in 2011, below the rate of inflation (HRSDC 2012: 3). Many have accepted at least one year of wage freezes, including members of the Canadian Union of Public Employees (CUPE) working for the City of Toronto who in 2012 were threatened with being locked out or having the employer impose terms and conditions of employment if they did not accept concessions (Grant 2012). Employers are also on the offensive against job security rights in collective agreements. Toronto municipal workers with permanent full-time positions are now only eligible for protection against contracting out after fifteen years of service rather than ten (ibid.). Some workers have also lost ground on pensions. For example, the federal government has now created a two-tier pension system for its workforce, with inferior provisions for new hires and all workers paying a larger share of contributions (May 2012).

The threat of job loss is a bludgeon that employers have used to pressure workers into giving concessions. The federal government is at the forefront of laying off public sector workers: close to 30,000 full-time equivalent positions will be eliminated between 2012 and 2015 (Macdonald 2012). Privatizing public services frequently leads to job losses, and privatization moves continue. For example, the Ontario government is planning to sell off ServiceOntario, which employs some 2,400 provincial employees (OPSEU 2012). Job cuts reduce union membership, leading to fewer activists and lowering dues income that finances union activities.

Many people who continue to work for governments or government-funded organizations are finding their jobs becoming more difficult as they attempt to deliver the same or greater levels of services with fewer people or simply experience heavier workloads. Precarious employment is spreading in the public sector (Stinson 2010). Employer work reorganization schemes usually have negative effects on workers, as research on Service Canada call centre work reveals (Pupo and Noack 2010). These problems for workers are not always recognized as threats to public sector unions as organizations. However, stressed-out, insecure and/or overworked workers may be less likely to volunteer for union activity. They may also blame "the union" for not protecting them or simply show no interest in a union they believe does nothing for them. Fearful workers may try to keep their jobs by trying to show their managers what flexible and hard-working individuals they are, thereby weakening union solidarity. Another challenge to unions is that members with precarious employment or stable but low-paid public sector jobs with few or no benefits may be hostile to unions because union officials have prioritized the interests of full-time workers with more secure jobs.

A threat of real importance to public sector unions is the hostility of many private sector workers toward them. Right-wing political appeals to "taxpayers" to support attacks on unionized public sector workers have had more success since the global economic crisis hit in 2007–08. Many workers in the overwhelmingly nonunionized private sector are experiencing growing insecurity in their paid work and personal lives. Only one quarter of private sector workers have workplace pensions; those who do are almost as likely to have a defined contribution plan as they are to have a defined benefit plan of the kind that a large majority of public sector workers enjoy (Canada/OSFI 2009). People who are struggling to cope with expenses and taxes that are rising faster than their incomes are often open to the argument that public sector workers do not deserve their relatively better benefits and rights. This idea has been actively promoted by many politicians, journalists, academics and think tank pundits. It has probably also gained more of a hearing because popular support for public education, health care and other services falls as the quantity and quality of public services decline and user fees are introduced or rise, leading more people to look to private companies for health care and education (Camfield 2012). Such hostility to public sector workers and their unions was very noticeable during the 2009 strike by Toronto municipal workers. Rob Ford tapped it successfully in his 2010 campaign for the mayor's office (Camfield 2011a: 23–29), and it contributed to the willingness of municipal workers to accept concessions in 2012.

This range of threats is daunting. Yet to fully appreciate them, it is necessary to understand why these dangers exist and are likely to become more severe in the years ahead. The problem is not just elected politicians hostile to the public sector and its unions, though they are very real. The problem is also more than the neoliberal ideology that justifies such politicians' actions as necessary and positive steps to reduce deficits and make the public sector smaller and more "efficient."[3]

These politicians and this ideology are part of a deeper process that has been underway internationally for over two decades: restructuring the public sector in order to turn broad welfare states into lean states geared to helping corporations and remaking societies in ways that boost profits in the era of neoliberal capitalism (Sears 1999; McBride and Whiteside 2011). This process has been advanced by governments formed by social democratic parties like Canada's New Democrats as well as by traditional parties of business (Evans 2012). For advocates of this project, the current global economic crisis is an opportunity to push the restructuring process further (Camfield 2011c; Fanelli and Hurl 2010; Huws 2011). Thus most of the threats that public sector unions face are ultimately caused by how capitalism itself is organized today (McNally 2011). The others stem from how working-class people are reacting to ever-harsher realities created by contemporary capitalism and from the relationship between unions as they currently exist and a divided and insecure working class.

UNION RENEWAL AND UNION POWER

Although union renewal has been discussed in many academic publications there is no agreement about what renewal means for unions. For example, some advocates of union renewal maintain that unions should form partnerships with employers. Others argue that unions should challenge employers and mobilize members and other people around a social justice vision to oppose neoliberalism.[4] A key question at the heart of discussions about union renewal — but rarely asked explicitly — is: What kind of unionism can and should be practiced today? In deciding how to answer this question, the issue of building power to respond to the threats unions face is paramount.

Two general kinds of unionism are practiced in the organizations to which the vast majority of public sector union members in Canada belong: social unionism and business unionism (Camfield 2011a: 50–52). Both are combinations of what active unionists do and what they believe their unions should try to do. Each is a distinctive approach to union activity and ideology (a mode of union praxis). Identifying a particular approach as dominant in a given union highlights important organizational features even if it does not tell us everything about the union (for one thing, there is variation in how a mode of unionism is practiced by specific groups of union members and staff [Ross 2012]).

Business unionism has a narrow focus on collective bargaining for union members and often adopts a cooperative approach to dealing with employers. Negotiating better wages and benefits is what really matters, though giving concessions in these and other aspects of bargaining is accepted as necessary. Business unionism accepts capitalist society as it exists today. At most, its supporters advocate small changes in law and policy. If the union gets involved in political action, it is generally limited to supporting individual candidates in elections or lobbying for legislative changes specific to their sectoral interests. Involvement with "the community" is limited to charity. For business unionists, unions should be run from the top down by officers and staff, with little membership involvement. This approach is common in local unions across Canada, including within parent unions in which social unionism is dominant. In the public sector, it is exemplified by unions like the Canadian Association of Professional Employees, the Association of Management, Administrative and Professional Crown Employees of Ontario and most unions of police officers, firefighters and university faculty.[5]

Social unionism's main differences with business unionism are its much greater concern for social and political issues not directly related to the workplace and a more critical attitude to neoliberal policies. Its supporters often rely on the same basic methods to achieve union goals: collective bargaining and parliamentary political action (which can include lobbying politicians and mounting campaigns designed to garner popular support as well as backing parties or candidates at election time). They sometimes go further and mobilize members and supporters in extraparliamentary political action such as demonstrations. Social unionists are more often than not nonconfrontational in their dealings with employers and governments. While they tend to be more willing than business unionists to mobilize members to advance their strategies, they are often wary of democratic membership control and militant tactics, such as occupations and political strikes. Social unionism is especially common in the largest public sector unions: CUPE, the National Union of Public and General Employees, the Public Service Alliance of Canada (PSAC) and the Fédération de la santé et des services sociaux (part of the Québec-based Confédération des syndicats nationaux).

How much power a group of unionized public sector workers has is determined by many factors. Some are for all intents and purposes largely or entirely beyond workers' ability to change in the foreseeable future, such as what kind of disruption is caused when they stop doing the work they are paid to do (which can be described as structural power) and what rights and restrictions labour law imposes on them. Others are much more subject to change. These include the degree of solidarity among a group of workers, their relationships of solidarity with other people, the way in which they understand society and their place in it, the union's financial and other material resources and the "aptitudes, competencies, abilities, social skills and know-how" of members and staff (Lévesque and Murray 2010: 341).

As Stephanie Ross (this volume) argues, the sources of structural power available to unionized public sector workers are not the same as those available to their counterparts in the private sector. Most public sector workers do not produce goods or services that are sold as commodities (although there are exceptions, mainly people who work for public utilities and Crown Corporations). As a result, when they strike or are locked out, their employers usually do not have to worry about falling revenues. On the contrary, employers may be glad to not have to pay workers' wages. What strikes by public sector workers have the specific potential to do is interrupt the provision of services and disrupt the operation of the state or other institutions in which they would otherwise be working. However, there are obstacles to actually being able to do this, especially legal restrictions on militant strike action. In addition, some public sector employers are willing and able to put up with a suspension of services in order to defeat unions. This makes the ability of public sector unionists to mobilize other people in their support an important source of power (Ross this volume).

If public sector workers are to maximize their power to contend with the threats they face, neither business unionism nor social unionism will do. One reason for this is that neither of these varieties of unionism is highly democratic, in the sense of making every effort to increase not just participation but also genuine membership control over union affairs. If workers do not control the union, it will be controlled by other people whose interests are not identical to theirs: full-time officers and staff or, worse, management. "The participation of members" is crucial for union power, "and it requires democracy to make members want to be involved" (Parker and Gruelle 1999: 14). An actively involved membership strengthens a union; in turn, evidence of union power encourages membership involvement. An inactive membership saps union power. This fuels a vicious circle because a weak union is less likely to encourage workers to commit their time and attention. The experience of democratically running an organization teaches people new skills, develops abilities and boosts self-confidence. This adds to their power, in part by making it easier for them to take advantage of whatever structural power they have. A democratic union culture that encourages people to speak up, raise tough questions and debate issues in a respectful way can strengthen unions. In such an environment, people are more likely to learn useful lessons from their inevitable mistakes and then be able to change how things are done (ibid.: 14–15; Camfield 2011a: 102–3).[6]

Another source of union power is the willingness of workers to engage in militant collective action. Militancy refers to assertive methods such as determined strikes, occupations, blockades and other kinds of direct action. This kind of collective action is much more likely to disrupt the operations of an employer or other opponent than activities such as passive, token picket lines or demonstrations that only mildly disturb anything or anyone. Militancy should not be equated with violence, as it often is by the corporate media. Supporters of both business unionism and social unionism often (though not always) reject more militant forms of action.

Solidarity among unionized workers and between them and other groups of people fighting for social justice is also important for union power. The most elementary kind of union solidarity is that which can exist between workers who belong to the same bargaining unit, are covered by the same collective agreement and deal with the same employer. This is rarely straightforward, since divisions can and do exist between workers in the same unit who do different kinds of work and between core and precariously employed workers. Broader union solidarity involves extending support to unionized workers in other bargaining units and other locals. Working-class solidarity reaches further, to other workers regardless of whether or not they are unionized. At its most wide-ranging, solidarity extends to supporting struggles by people who may be part of the working class but who are taking action around issues not directly connected to paid work, such as students trying to block tuition increases or people opposing cuts to services for refugees, and to oppressed people who are not part of the working class, such as self-employed indigenous people in rural areas. Business unionism cultivates only the most elementary kind of solidarity. Practicing social unionism is more likely to foster broader forms of solidarity, given social unionism's greater concern with issues not directly related to the workplace and its more critical view of neoliberalism. However, the potential power of solidarity is limited when supporters of social unionism do not engage in extraparliamentary political action and shy away from militant ways of expressing solidarity.

How workers understand society and their place in it can affect how much power they wield. For example, unionists who can analyze how specific moves by employers are part of a global process of "reforming" the public sector that harms workers and services are unlikely to make the mistake of endorsing management schemes that are part of the neoliberal restructuring agenda.[7] Such union members are also more likely to try to build broader bonds of solidarity with people who use public services. Recognizing that attacks on the public sector stem from capitalism, not just from individual politicians or one specific political party, helps to prevent reliance on false or fair-weather friends. Recognizing the stakes in a strike or lockout can bolster the resolve to resist. People who interpret setbacks as part of a long-term struggle are less likely to give up on unions after a defeat. When it comes to this source of power, business unionism offers very little to workers because it fundamentally accepts the status quo in society. Social unionism usually offers more. Yet in contemporary Canada it almost never involves analysis that digs deep to really grasp how capitalism works and how best to resist capital's offensive (Camfield 2011a).

AN ALTERNATIVE: SOCIAL MOVEMENT UNIONISM

Viewed from the perspective of what kind of unionism is best suited to enhancing the power of public sector workers, the two approaches that together characterize the vast majority of union activity across Canada today are inadequate. Fortunately, business unionism and social unionism are not the only possibilities for workers. A very different approach, social movement unionism, has more potential (Camfield 2007).

Social movement unionism is committed to militancy and solidarity among unions and between unions and other social justice organizations in a struggle for progressive social change that involves extraparliamentary action. Crucially, it puts democracy at the heart of unionism. Its supporters believe that unions should be run by active memberships and see democracy as key to building workers' power. Social movement unionism has some presence in CUPW. It is also practiced by small numbers of activists in CUPE and by individuals scattered across other unions.[8]

By making democracy central and striving for militancy and far-reaching solidarity, social movement unionism boosts union power. Its commitment to fighting for social change in the streets and in the workplace, breaking out of the confines of relying on parliamentary political action, has the same effect. This commitment by its supporters also tends to make them more open to critical ways of understanding society and to questioning influential inherited ideas in the union movement, such as the belief that unions cannot successfully defy the law.

Public sector workers who want to do everything possible to increase union power and thereby improve their odds in the high-stakes struggle against austerity and restructuring should practice social movement unionism. In this, they will be more likely to be successful when they clearly link the defence of public sector workers' pay, benefits and working conditions with the defence of the services they deliver and the people who use those services. They will also tend to do better when they take into account that most users of public services are often nonunionized private sector workers whose generally worse conditions "leav[e] public sector workers open to resentment" (Hurley and Gindin 2011) in this era of austerity and scapegoating. These public sector workers must also take into account that the racial composition of the public sector workforce is often "whiter" than the overall population.[9]

An unfortunate reality about public services as they exist in this capitalist society is that they are often inadequate and unresponsive to the needs of those who use them. Public education at all levels, for example, has been suffering because of underfunding. For many students school is boring and stifling. Schools, universities and colleges also tend to reflect and perpetuate the racism, colonialism, sexism and heterosexism of the society of which they are a part (Sears 2003). To take another example, people who use social welfare services are often treated in demeaning and hostile ways. Another unfortunate reality is that the jobs of some "back office" public sector workers involve providing services to top managers and governments that are of little or no benefit to the bulk of the population.

These problems are one reason why support for public services and public sector workers is not stronger than it is. There is an important lesson in this for those who want to change and strengthen public sector unions: it is not enough to defend public services and jobs. A perspective of improving and changing the public sector is also needed. An alternative approach to public sector unionism needs an alternative vision of the public sector. To have an impact, this vision must lead to action. As two advocates of this orientation argue, "Our commitment must be proven in practice, through the priorities we set and carry out" (Hurley and Gindin 2011). What this means will be different for, say, university teachers than for child welfare workers or support workers in health care. CUPW's demands in its 2010–2011 round of bargaining for expanding Canada Post's range of services to include financial services were an example of trying to tailor this orientation to the post office (CUPW 2010).[10]

But regardless of where they work, supporters of social movement unionism face the challenge of developing strategies and tactics to resist concession demands, address precarious employment and other divisions among workers, fight for a better, different public sector and support other struggles against injustice. This will inevitably involve innovating and experimenting with forms of collective action that are uncommon in unions in Canada today. There are many possibilities. Inspiration can come from the history of the working-class movement, from other contemporary movements like the 2012 Québec student movement (Lafrance and Sears 2012) and from other countries. To give just two examples: going door to door to build support for demands that would change the public sector (as postal workers did in Halifax in 2011 [Bleakney 2011]) and occupations of workplaces or other sites.

As activists grapple with this complex challenge, they would be wise to remember a lesson shared by a private sector unionist that is just as relevant in the public sector: "Workplace success is what enables broader social struggle ... We must be able to mobilize workers in the workplace in order to mobilize them on social issues" (Johnston 2008: 12). In addition, because most public sector workers are women, who experience sexism on and off the job, activists can benefit by adopting innovative analysis and practices developed by feminist unionists that can make "workplace success" more likely (Briskin 2011a). To allow activists to challenge the racial oppression and privilege that weaken unions, supporters of social movement unionism must also integrate antiracism into their approach.

HOW TO CHANGE THE UNIONS?[11]

No argument about a new direction for public sector unionism can be very useful if it fails to answer the question of how this direction can be implemented in the here and now. Over the last several decades, people who want to make unions more militant and active as a force for social change have usually tried to try to get leftists elected to high-ranking office and hired into influential staff jobs in order to reform unions from above. This approach is incompatible with social movement unionism, because it treats the development of greater democratic control of unions by an active membership as at best of secondary importance and at worst as irrelevant. It has also failed on its own terms, as the rightward evolution of the Canadian Auto Workers' leadership demonstrates (Camfield 2011a: 116) and as some left-wing public sector union veterans have concluded.[12]

Another road to changing unions exists: reform from below. This involves fostering social movement unionism at the rank-and-file level by starting to do unionism differently, in more militant, democratic and solidaristic ways. Activists are much more likely to be successful at this when they suggest practical ways of responding to the concerns of their coworkers that are potentially more effective than what official leaders are doing. In other words, the starting point should be today's concrete issues, not an abstract program for social movement unionism.

From the reform from below perspective, electing members to union office is a tactic for advancing social movement unionism, never an end in itself. One reason why winning union elections cannot be the central tactic for transforming unions is that reform-oriented union officials are subject to strong conservative pressures from other union officers and staff, employers and the state. Another is that for "radicals who take office without a mobilized base to support them ... union democracy becomes a hindrance to the union acting on a 'social justice' program" (Weiner 2012). Officers intent on change are less likely to stray from the course if they are accountable to organized rank-and-file workers committed to social movement unionism. Thus it is crucial to build a base of active members who understand and advocate this approach. Success in doing this can be aided by trying to develop the capacities of rank-and-file activists, who are often important informal leaders. Fostering collective responsibility and decision-making instead of looking to heroic individuals can also be helpful, including when reformers are elected to formal leadership positions (Briskin 2011b).

The bureaucratic character of labour unions makes it important for members working for change from below to organize themselves independently, outside of official union structures. Organizing this way helps activists to take initiatives, push for change within the union and hold fellow activists who are elected to union office accountable. Looking south to the U.S., the Caucus of Rank-and-File Educators (CORE) shows what this can look like. CORE was formed in 2008 by members of the Chicago Teachers' Union (CTU) who wanted to fight school closures when the CTU's top officers did not. CORE members allied themselves with parents and other people active around defending and changing schools. At the same time they organized teachers around workplace issues and changing the CTU to make it a more democratic and fighting union. CORE pledged itself to opposing the neoliberal education policies pushed by school managers and the Obama administration and backed by the top officials of the American Federation of Teachers. In the 2010 CTU elections, CORE supporters defeated the entrenched leadership group and took the helm of the union (Sustar 2010). In 2012, 92 percent of the members of the CORE-led CTU took part in its strike vote and an astonishing 98 percent of those who voted cast ballots authorizing a strike (Ashby 2012). The efforts of CORE activists were crucial to the successful CTU strike of September 2012 (Brogan 2012).

It is rare for people who practice social movement unionism to so quickly achieve as much as CORE has. Public sector unions may well suffer grave defeats before efforts to build workers' power in new ways start to take shape. When they do, those involved will be better equipped for success if they clearly understand what they are up against, how much public sector unionism needs to change and what path offers the possibility of making that kind of change as part of the broader reinvention of the working-class movement that is urgently needed.

Notes

1. Thanks to Cindy McCallum-Miller, Brian McDougall, Stephanie Ross, Larry Savage and other contributors to this book for their comments.
2.. Even if parts of such laws are eventually struck down by the courts it is wrong to think that the 2007 Supreme Court of Canada ruling (*B.C. Health Services* 2007) that extended limited Charter of Rights and Freedoms protection to the process of collective bargaining provides public sector unions with a strong shield. See Fudge 2012. In 2012 the Ontario government introduced a bill that would have banned strikes across the public sector, restricted arbitrators' rulings and allowed the government to freeze or roll back wages and benefits until the provincial budget deficit is eliminated (Walkom 2012). However, the bill fell off the order paper when the legislature was prorogued.
3. On this ideology, see Beitel 2010; Camfield 2011c; Shields and Evans 1998.
4. For a survey, see Kumar and Schenk 2006.
5. See Savage and Webber, this volume, for a specific discussion of the varieties of unionism practiced by unions of "professionals."
6. A recent example from a different social movement is relevant here: highly participatory democratic student unions were a key reason why in 2012 Québec students were able to sustain their strike and in May reject a deal that was widely seen as inadequate (see Lafrance and Sears 2012).
7. For example, the leadership of the Saskatchewan Union of Nurses has endorsed "a collaborative approach to utilizing lean principles in order to transform the health care system" (SUN/SAHO 2012: 1). On lean work reorganization in health care, see Armstrong and Armstrong 2010.
8. This draws on Camfield (2011a: 51), where social movement unionism as understood here is also distinguished from other approaches that are wrongly confused with it.
9. On the federal government see PSAC 2012d.
10. See also the recent efforts of the Chicago Teachers Union (Brogan 2012).
11. Ideas in this section are explored at greater length in Camfield 2011a: 111–41.
12. At a meeting in Ottawa in early 2012 that brought together several dozen labour leftists, mainly CUPE, PSAC and CUPW staff, there was much self-criticism about the failure of this model (email from Brian McDougall to author, March 18, 2012).

6. UNIONS IN THE NONPROFIT SOCIAL SERVICES SECTOR

Gendered Resistance

Donna Baines

Though often thought of as insignificant compared to the private and public sectors, welfare state downsizing and contracting-out has positioned the nonprofit sector as an increasingly important player in service provision and employment (Cunningham 2008; Shields, Evans and Richmond 2005). Governments around the globe have off-loaded public sector work to the nonprofit sector because costs, primarily wages and benefits, are consistently much lower. Since roughly the 1980s, the nonprofit services sector has simultaneously been a site of: (a) pro-market restructuring; (b) collective and individual resistance; and (c) as part of this resistance, a site in which alternative forms of unionism have been mobilized (Baines 2010a; 2010b).

This chapter begins with a quick portrait of the nonprofit social services sector (NPSS) with attention to: the predominantly female and increasingly racialized labour force; gendered social expectations of the workforce's commitment to endless care regardless of working conditions or wages; and some of the ways that the ethos of care shapes the identities of the workforce and the kinds of resistance mobilized in this sector. While the workforce is not wholly composed of "angels of mercy," as they are often portrayed, workers have a mandate to care and a work culture that fosters self-exploitation and the sense of being part of a moral project. The latter part of the chapter analyzes some of the ways that workers in the nonprofit sector have used their unions to improve their conditions of work as well as to challenge larger agendas impacting on the public and nonprofit sectors.

OVERVIEW OF THE NONPROFIT SOCIAL SERVICES

To itself, the nonprofit sector tends to mean agencies and organizations that have an ethic of service to others and operate outside both the profit motive and direct government control and provision (Van Til 2000). However, the ethic of service can take on very right or left political purposes, with nonprofit services ranging from anti-abortion counselling to radical action collectives. Similarly, nonprofits involve a vast array of entities, including large sporting facilities such as the YMCA/YWCAs worldwide; chains of nonprofit services such as long-term care centres; and large and small, local, community-based services such as settlement houses, soup kitchens, women's shelters and child-care centres.

Good statistical data is hard to come by concerning the nonprofit sector. Though Statistics Canada has fairly good data on charities, 40 percent of nonprofits are not charities, and these nonprofits are often the smaller and/or more politicized services, such as antiviolence services and union-linked action centres for unemployed people. The procedures for registering as a charity are fairly burdensome, and many smaller agencies do not have the time or resources, while agencies that see advocacy and social justice as part of their mandate tend to forgo charitable status due to its restrictions on political activism.

Similarly, Statistics Canada data on nonprofits is problematic as it includes large entities such as hospitals, universities and colleges. Though technically part of the nonprofit sector as they are run by public boards and do not generate surplus, the workforce in these large organizations tends to have public sector mandates, funding, wage levels, benefits, pensions and working conditions, skewing statistics upwardly and distorting the portrait of the nonprofit sector. Canada-wide, most nonprofits have fewer than twenty employees (Clutterbuck and Howarth 2007) and very different ethos and conditions than hospitals, colleges and universities.

Notwithstanding these problems with the data, the Canadian Centre for Social Development (Scott and Struthers 2006) provides one of the better profiles of the nonprofit sector, noting that it employs 1.2 million people in 69,000 organizations. Interestingly, half of these 69,000 organizations are very small groups in Ontario; 50 percent has fewer than five employees while only 6 percent has over one hundred employees (Clutterbuck and Howarth 2007). Depending on the statistics used, the nonprofit sector is 6 to 11 percent of Canada's workforce (Statistics Canada 2003; Scott et al. 2006), making it the same size as trades, larger than professions and roughly the same size as manufacturing (10 percent) and private services (12 percent) (Scott and Struthers 2006). Though the nonprofit sector prides itself on its independence from government and market, some agencies receive more than 90 percent of funding from government while other agencies providing the same type of services receive less than 50 percent (Charlesworth 2010).

Prior to neoliberalism, the nonprofit sector was not merely an extension of the public sector, existing instead to provide alternative services for specific and new populations and to act as an advocate for those less heard. Under neoliberalism, the nonprofit social services sector has grown significantly because of the cost savings to governments in terms of wages and overhead. The NPSS currently acts as a low-wage drag on the public sector that will likely continue to grow as governments attempt to undercut and downsize public services.

As Cunningham and James (2010) note, most care work in the nonprofits cannot be off-shored to other regions; it has to be provided in a hands-on, immediate way, making care work an area of the economy that requires an ongoing locally-situated workforce. Though the work cannot be globalized, the workforce can, and every year temporary workers are brought to Canada to work as nannies and caregivers for elderly and dependent adults, providing a vulnerable and exploitable workforce and keeping care wages low. The paid care workforce in the nonprofits is increasingly racialized, particularly in large urban centres (Clutterbuck and Howarth 2007), a further manifestation of the global movement of women in search of employment and the lower quality of jobs made available to racialized women (Hochschild and Ehrenreich 2003).

UNIQUE ASPECTS: CARE, ALTRUISM, SOCIAL JUSTICE

While the private sector operates on a profit motive and the public sector purportedly runs on a public service mandate, the nonprofit sector claims to have a unique ethos combining service to others, altruism and broad social participation (Van Til 2000). A number of critics argue that the ethos of the nonprofit sector is more aspirational than something that can be seen in daily practice, and service users certainly express frustration with the care they receive (McDonald and Marston 2002). However, many workers assert that the opportunity to work in tandem with one's values somewhat compensates for lower wages and difficult working conditions (Nickson et al. 2008; Cunningham 2008) and is consistently reported as the key aspect of work that draws people to and retains staff in the nonprofit sector (Baines 2010a; Van Til 2000).

The largest subsector of the nonprofit sector is social services where a mandate to "care" predominates (Charlesworth 2010), taking on the flavour of social justice in agencies more explicitly committed to social equity, while the provision of high quality care is the mantra in less socially conscious agencies. Relationships between and among people are thought to form the basis of good care, while themes of self-determination, diversity, inclusion and social participation are often present in varying degrees, differing from agency to agency and between different kinds of services.

As noted earlier, the workforce is highly gendered — approximately 75 percent female (Saunders 2008) — and work culture, worker identities and collective and individual resistance are similarly gendered. In order to avoid essentializing women in discussions of women, leadership and unions, Briskin (2006) recommends the use of a materialist/social constructionist framework that begins with the realities of women's lives in the home, community and workplace.

Rather than a set of skills and knowledge, care work is generally seen as a "natural" extension of the kinds of tasks women undertake in the home and community, making it hard to increase the status or pay of this work (Themundo 2009). Particularly in the nonprofit sector, which involves a large portion of volunteer as well as paid workers, the lines become very blurry between paid care work and unpaid care work that is altruistically provided by "caring" citizens as a way to "give back" or fight inequity (Baines 2004). Studies confirm that the predominantly female care workers choose to work in the nonprofit sector because of the opportunity to work in tandem with their values of care and/or social justice (Baines 2010a; Van Til 2000). While laudable, these values and this choice are gendered, socially conditioned and socially constructed, as are the expectations workers and managers have that the predominantly female staff will undertake additional hours to extend and expand the services provided to clients and communities. These lines of tensions form the backdrop to work and resistance in the nonprofit sector.

Interestingly, nonprofit workers also tend to undertake many types of unpaid work at their own workplaces — they work through lunch breaks, work late, take work home, work on weekends, evenings and vacations, take clients home with them or on vacation and bring goods from home and family members in to help out (Baines 2004; 2006). The majority of this overtime is unpaid and not formally recognized or documented, though managers rely on it to keep resource-stretched agencies solvent (Baines 2010a). Much of this unpaid work has a unique aspect of resistance to it; many workers report they cannot feel comfortable with themselves if they know that service users or communities are in difficulty and they have not tried to help.

While it is normative and essentialist to assume endless care from a particular population such as women, it is, of course, not wrong to care. Unions and other social justice movements would be far better off if more people displayed care, solidarity and a willingness to improve the lot of others. However, when this "boundaryless" and elastic care is compulsory and assumed by employers to be an extension of women's "natural" capacities, it is a form of exploitation and should be resisted. When undertaken consciously (and critically) as a response to an uncaring agency or larger society, this self-sacrifice can be seen as a form of resistance, a source of power and a base from which to organize.

Union activism sometimes forms part of the resistance strategies in the NPSS. Nonprofit sector workers that I have interviewed for various studies consistently report that they turned to union activism because ongoing waves of restructuring made them feel that they had "lost their voice" at work and needed a new vehicle through which to address injustices in the workplace and larger society. I will return to this theme later in the chapter.

UNIONS IN THE NONPROFIT SECTOR

Most Canadian unions see themselves as social unions[1] — representing members at the bargaining table while simultaneously organizing on issues such as the environment, social programs, violence against women, health care, immigration and world peace and international issues (Schenk 2003; Ross 2007, 2011). Robinson (1993: 21) argues that social unionism operates in a unique way in Canada, unfolding within a certain "moral economy" in which members are attracted, retained and mobilized by invoking "the importance of moral commitments of labour-movement members, leaders, and supporters." This moral economy overlaps well with the moral economy of NPSS workers who, as noted earlier, are attracted to the sector because of the opportunities to "live [their] values." Social unionism is the official discourse of most of the unions representing workers in the nonprofit sector, among which some of the largest are the Canadian Union of Public Employees, provincial affiliates of the National Union of Public and General Employees, the Canadian Auto Workers and the Service Employees International Union.

Some claim that social unionism can be a form of community development in which the global and the local come together, and the interests of those within and those outside the union meld into activist campaigns that revitalize civil society, meet growing social needs and experiment with new forms of democratic participation (Coulter 2011; Ross 2011; Tufts 1998). However, others caution that social unionism is often a top-down practice in which elected union officials and staff promote the ideals of social unionism, involving members in policy decisions and formal mobilizations but rarely undertaking sustained, grassroots organizing or mobilization (Black 2005).

RESTRUCTURING AND MANAGERIALISM

The beginning of neoliberalism in the mid 1980s marked a dramatic change in social service organization, entitlement and delivery (Teeple 2000; Cohen 1997). Globally, governments cut funds to public services and encouraged citizens to rely on themselves, their families and the private market to meet their human service needs (Clarke 2004; Teeple 2000). Ongoing waves of funding cuts from governments meant that services were under-resourced, overstretched and redesigned. Public and nonprofit services also took on a new character, promoting, legitimizing and emulating the virtues of the private market while remaining putatively nonmarket (Baines 2010a), providing services for a variety of publics (Clarke 2004).

Globally, a management model known as New Public Management or "managerialism" accompanied neoliberalism and was introduced to the nonprofits through government contract requirements (Shields, Evans and Richmond 2005). Though touted by the right as a mechanism to improve "taxpayer accountability," improve efficiency and cut costs, labour process theory has tended to view managerialism as a form of work standardization and intensification, transferring increased control to management and decreasing worker autonomy through rigid performance measures and requirements to meet government standards for accreditation, professionalization and various other metrics of cost control, quality assurance and outcomes (Baines 2004, 2010b; Cunningham 2008). Many social justice-oriented practices fall outside the standardized outcome measures, making it hard for many nonprofit workers to find the space for the kind of work they want to undertake (Baines 2010a).

PRECARIOUS WORK

Though neoliberalism and managerialism have entered the nonprofit sector in the last two decades, precarious work has a very long history in the nonprofit sector with contract and part-time work being the most prevalent types of work (McMullen and Schellenberg 2002). Neoliberal restructuring of labour markets encouraged nonprofit sector employers to introduce "flexible" forms of work, including "thin" staffing such as solo shifts; lean shifts (one or two workers per site, sometimes with cell phone access to workers or supervisors at other sites); split shifts (wherein staff work an hour or two in the morning and return in the evening for a few more hours of work); part-time, contract, casual and other forms of temporary work; and expanded reliance on volunteer work (Baines 2004; Cunningham 2008). Largely funded by time-limited government contracts or charitable grants, funding for nonprofit agencies tends to be tied to discrete projects with clear start and end dates, prescribing a certain wage and benefit level and resulting in staff layoffs if contracts are not renewed (Clutterbuck and Howarth 2007). Given the time-limited nature of the funding, permanent work is increasingly less common. Under this kind of funding regime, monies for infrastructure are rare, and there is no way to increase wages or benefits except through private fundraising — a very resource-intensive and precarious endeavour (Charlesworth 2010).

In some cases, government funding explicitly structures nonprofit work to be part-time — such as in home care, many jobs in immigrant and refugee services and youth work — and agencies have little power to change this. In other areas, inadequate funding pushes agencies to turn to part-time, casual, contract and other forms of precarious work. The current forms of precarious work in the nonprofits represents a loss of pensions and benefits, with certain groups of workers — such as home care and services for children and youth — even less likely to have benefits, job security, sick leave, annual leave or union representation. Rather than rupturing the relationship between employee and employer to the point where workers are no longer willing to work extra unpaid hours, precarious workers are particularly vulnerable to expectations that they should self-sacrifice for service users and the agency in which they are employed (Baines 2004).

RESISTANCE AND NEW UNION FORMS

Aptheker (1989) argues that, for many women, resistance flows from the social conditions and spaces that are available to them. This chapter argues that the resistance of NPSS workers needs to be assessed from within the highly gendered context in which care work is performed. Resistance, paid and unpaid work spill over into other spheres in messy and permeable ways, as do the values and emotions behind them. This means that the resistance undertaken by nonprofit workers often looks different and contains different aspects than resistance in other, less gendered contexts.

For example, unlike industrial workers, NPSS employees often blame governments and wider uncaring society rather than their employers for problems in the workplace including low wages, difficult working conditions, poor services and larger wrongs perpetrated against service users and communities (Carniol 2010). Similarly, workplace resistance, including union demands, often targets multiple and somewhat abstract powers rather than focusing on specific employers as the exclusive or even the primary target (Ross 2011; Smith 2007). Collected as part of a larger project on unionization in the nonprofit social services, the quote below highlights the broad, politicized way that many nonprofit workers frame the social problems and the permeability of their workdays.

> Our work doesn't stop at the end of the day or at the door of the agency. We bring the world in with us to work and the world walks through those doors every day looking for help and assistance. It's only natural that we would get involved in activist work in this city — heck, activist work in this world, 'cause it sure never needed it more. (Baines 2010a: 20)

Some overlap exists between resistance strategies used by public and nonprofit sector workers. For example, some workers in both settings participate in advocacy for clients and bend or downplay rules that disadvantage service users (Carniol 2010; Lundy 2011). However, in an effort to manage and minimize risk, public sector workers and some nonprofit workers (mainly those providing government-funded and -mandated services such as probation or child welfare) are highly managerialized and generally so tightly scripted that it is more difficult for them to find the time to contemplate, let alone challenge, larger social justice issues in the workplace (Baines 2006; Lundy 2011). In contrast, the missions of most nonprofit social services provide NPSS workers, who are generally less constrained by managerialism than their public sector cohorts, with an "official" if not an actualized mandate for collective social justice strategies on behalf of clients and communities.

The study of unionization in the nonprofit sector referred to earlier (Baines 2010a) also contained data showing that a number of nonprofit workers developed individual and collective resistance strategies in response to decreased worker autonomy and increased management control of the labour process. Staff meetings and other collective forums for staff are viewed as inefficiencies that agencies can no longer afford and are reduced or eliminated. The curtailment of collective forums and the reduction or elimination of other kinds of social justice practices (as mentioned earlier) led many workers to report that they feel they have "lost their voice" in agency issues and experienced a serious reduction in the meaningfulness of their work content. To regain their voice, some workers turned to various workplace practices that challenged agency policies and the larger popular culture of "cutbacks and uncaring" (Baines 2010b). These resistance practices included: encouraging service users to advocate for themselves even where it involved risk to the worker; bending rules and looking for other ways to get service users all they are entitled to and more; taking on many hours of unpaid work in their own agencies and others; organizing service user groups outside their workplaces; building coalitions with social movements and agencies; providing new and innovative services for free; and using unions as vehicles for social justice. These practices were sources of meaning for many nonprofit workers, and as one research participant noted, "If you haven't got meaning in these jobs, what else have you got?" (Baines 2010b: 490).

Similarly, the union local president in a mid-sized, multiservice agency made explicit links between the lack of voice workers experience in the workplace and the priority nonprofit workers place on it.

> Wages and working conditions are always important to our members, but people really want a voice in how decisions get made. We have expertise in our program areas, we know our clients and communities, and we want some say in how things get done. (Baines 2010a: 19)

Many nonprofit activists tended to be interested in ways of working within unions that were consistent with nonprofit values and practices such as broad participation, collective problem solving and giving back — hallmarks of the voluntary spirit (Baines 2010a, 2010b). For example, one activist reported that her local always had more people wanting to run for office than positions available. The local decided to create a system of shadow executive positions and shadow stewards wherein two people could share one position, undertaking the roles and responsibilities jointly. In another example, a local initiated a "buddy system" in which newer activists were twinned with experienced ones to share skills and knowledge, drawing more people into "the life of the local." A third local described a similar situation in which "alternate positions" were developed, creating a pathway for drawing new people into leadership roles. In a fourth example, a union president noted that she and her fellow activists drew on their experience in community activism and mass movements to create a local that was formally hierarchical (to meet the requirements of the parent union's constitution) but operated more or less on a consensus basis, providing opportunities for all members to have a voice and to influence priorities and activities (Baines 2010b).

Developing a collective and participatory ethos, another local union president spoke of maintaining a core of activists who worked very hard to maintain a local spirit that was "creative, effective, and very positive, not negative and draggy." Their goal was to craft "an oasis for the members" or positive space to counteract the alienation associated with working in an increasingly managerialized workplace (Baines 2010a). These alternate practices are aspects of what Briskin (2011b) calls post heroic leadership, in which power is shared, relationships are built and authority is downplayed. They are also consistent with the idealized nonprofit values of full social participation, equity and care (Van Til 2000).

Reflecting the nonprofit ethos of social justice, my data also shows that unions worked with a variety of actors in the nonprofit sector and beyond to build new initiatives and promote social justice. For example, some executive directors reported feeling restricted by new funding and managerial regimes, and like their staff, they were interested in pursuing new forms of voice and participation. In this case, a joint coalition of nonprofit social service employers, staff, service users and unions formed to challenge funding inequities. The coalition was consensus-based and, while trust was initially difficult to establish between some employers and union people, one union representative noted that nonprofit services tend to be "full of problem solvers and peacemakers who help smooth the rough parts around relationships, even those that are typically contentious" (Baines 2010a: 14). During the months that it existed, the coalition was viewed as a model of what could be achieved if multiple players in the sector worked together toward social equity goals.

Ross (2011) argues that, rather than a stark dichotomy, social unionism (a focus on wider social justice) and business unionism (a focus on servicing and collective bargaining) should be understood in the context of individual and larger union struggles as tactics that can stretch beyond the immediate benefit of members. In a classic example of using collective bargaining as a way to improve working conditions and the quality of care provided to service users, La Rose (2009) analyzes a recent strike at a large nonprofit social service (child welfare) agency where the major strike demand was caps on caseload sizes and improved wording around workload size. Neoliberal restructuring had replaced the more open-ended relationship-building processes previously used in this sector with highly standardized and circumscribed work practices, including computerized tick-box assessment tools and closely monitored timelines for the completion of pre-set tasks. At the time of the strike, government funding was tied to pre-set timelines (benchmarks) for task completion, leaving workers feeling highly scrutinized, deskilled, exhausted and like they had little or no capacity to provide care for their clients. Though the strike lasted six weeks, the local returned to work having won their issues and set a precedent for child welfare locals across the province, which other locals quickly adopted (La Rose 2009: 241). The new collective agreement wording not only improved social workers' quality of work life through smaller caseloads but also improved care for service users though the same gain.

Though strikes have the potential to deeply divide a workforce, La Rose (2009: 240) notes that this strike gave child welfare workers the opportunity to build relationships across departments, in effect coming out of their silos and gaining a broader understanding of issues faced by workers across the entire agency. La Rose also reports that each picket line had its own character — one focused on singing, eventually forming a choir and recording a CD, while another emphasized fun and irreverence, featuring a "bring your pet to the picket" day, a pajama day and a "makeover on the picket line" day. Reflecting the shared social justice values of the sector, some managers were supportive throughout the strike, while others gained a new appreciation for their staff after taking on the work of frontline jobs during the six-week strike.

CONCLUSIONS

The current context of economic austerity will present deep challenges to unions and the nonprofit sector as a whole. Recent findings suggest that it is not only market forces but also a larger cultural shift toward extended public sector austerity that sets the boundaries for management-union struggles in the NPSS. As Peters and Masaoka (2000: 316) note, the same factors — government cutbacks, increased community need, greater competition for funds — create both the conditions for union activism and the pressure on management to oppose it. However, as Godard (2011) points out, union resistance is part of the fabric and structure of capitalism, rather than something to which a particular sector or group of managers and workers can chart a completely different course despite claims to an ethos of participation and a higher moral project. Godard (2012: 298) argues further that collective mani-festation of conflict can be expected to not just return, but to change as well.

Cunningham and James (2010: 35–36) note that a number of strategies have been put forward in order to attract a workforce facing organizational, sectoral and labour market challenges and to increase union density in the nonprofit sector, including "workplace and 'beyond the enterprise' elements." The discussion in this chapter shows that both social unionist (beyond the enterprise) and business unionist (workplace) strategies have been used by nonprofit union activists to challenge the stinginess of managerialism and to build vibrant locals that act as a counterculture to the alienation of the neolib-eral work environment. The alternative structures and strategies discussed in this chapter provide strong examples of practices that resonate with the care and inclusion values held by most of those employed in the nonprofit sector and form the basis of union power in the sector. Union locals are willing to modify union structures that do not meet members' needs and to find ways to tap into workers' sense that they are part of a moral endeavor in which defense of service users, the community and each other is pivotal. Finally, as noted earlier, the values of social unionism and its democratic manifestations are consistent with the best of the social justice ethos of the nonprofit sec-tor — participatory decision making, community mobilization and mutual empowerment. Despite austerity and the attack on public sector wages and conditions, this complex set of factors will likely continue to make social unionism an appealing choice for nonprofit workers and provides unions with an opening for further unionization and social justice in this growing sector.

Note

1. Rather than a stark dichotomy, Kumar and Murray (2003) argue that in reality, business and social unionism comfortably coexist within most Canadian unions and meet members' needs in different but important ways. See also Ross 2011.

7. IN THE PUBLIC INTEREST

Nurses on Strike[1]

Linda Briskin

This chapter[2] explores the emergence of a militant discourse among nurses focused on the public interest, what I call the politicization of caring, which has supported a new approach to the ethics of striking. This discourse emphasizes patient care and calls for the revaluing of the expertise and caring involved in nurses' work. The politicization of caring has created the conditions for widespread public support for nurses' strikes and offers a paradigm that supports the expansion rather than the narrowing of the collective bargaining agenda. This chapter suggests that public sector strikes may offer vehicles to renew unions, build community support for public services and challenge legislative and employer attacks on collective bargaining.

NURSING WORK AND HEALTH CARE RESTRUCTURING

In the 1960s and 1970s, amid widespread public sector union organizing, nurses formed unions separate from their professional associations.[3] However, by the late 1970s, like many other public sectors, health care began to face government cutbacks in funding, wage freezes, reduction in services/downsizing, intensification, "rationalization" and fragmentation of work, labour shortages, privatization and public-private partnerships (P3), contracting out of cleaning and food services and the transformation of a large proportion of work from relatively secure full-time employment to part-time, casual, temporary and often precarious employment.

> Nurses' work settings are now characterized by intensification of patient care, acceleration of change in technology and treatment regimes, shortages of nurses, rationalization of work, and severe cost-cutting measures. Moreover, nurses frequently experience feelings of powerlessness in the system, lack of respect, verbal and

physical abuse [and] unsatisfactory management practices. (Hibberd 1992: 588)

Provincial governments spend around 35 percent of total expenditures on health care, with a high of 40.3 percent in Alberta and a low of 16.6 percent in the Yukon in 2010.[4] In 2006, compensation represented 60 percent of the total hospital budgets, a decline from a high of 75 percent in the late 1970s (Mackenzie and Rachlis 2010: 10). Since health-care jobs are less susceptible to outsourcing (Clark and Clark 2006: 51), pressures to reduce labour costs have been relentless.[5] Although doctors' salaries represent a disproportionate amount of these expenditures, nursing work has faced particularly acute reorganization and restructuring.

Nursing work, then, faces the austerity measures and the private sector managerial approaches forced on all public sector arenas. In fact, nursing work offers a snapshot of such work reorganization, especially the move from full-time to part-time and contract work that is so characteristic of neoliberal economies. In 2009, only 58.6 percent of Canadian registered nurses worked full time, 30.6 percent worked part time and 10.7 percent worked casual and often precarious hours.[6] Two thirds juggle multiple jobs. Perhaps uniquely, the employment relations in nursing work are compounded by the dual pressures of nurse shortages and pressures to work overtime, often unpaid.

Like other arenas of just-in-time production, casual nurses are called in only when needed and are cheaper because they receive no benefits. In *Negotiations '99: Stand Up for Nursing*, the Saskatchewan Union of Nurses (SUN 1999: 1) stressed that the nursing shortage is "forcing nurses to work mandatory overtime. Nurses are suffering extreme stress, leading to many more nurses suffering work-related injuries and chronic illness." At the same time, "increasing 'casualization' of the nursing workforce" means that "instead of staffing properly with full-time and regular part-time nurses, management uses casual nurses to staff for heavy shifts, or 'peak hours,' just like fast food outlets. For the remainder of the shift, patient care [is] at risk" (SUN 1999: 3).

Research commissioned by the Canadian Nurses Association shows that 20 percent of new nurses walk away because of poor working conditions, low wages and a shortage of full-time work caused by downsizing and cost-cutting. Furthermore, earnings for nursing graduates are actually declining (Picard 2000). As a result, there is a growing shortage of nurses. The 2011 shortfall of 22,000 nurses "is masked only by delayed retirements and heavy workloads" and the Canadian Federation of Nurses Unions (CFNU) predicts a shortfall of 60,000 full-time equivalent nurses by 2022. Such shortages have translated into a dramatic pattern of overtime work. "Public sector nurses worked 20,627,800 hours of overtime in 2010, the equivalent of 11,400 jobs; almost 15 percent of nurses did not get paid for their overtime hours" (CFNU

2012: 3–4). The number of overtime hours is also increasing. "In 1987, RNs [registered nurses] worked 144,600 overtime hours per week, while in 2008, RNs worked 412,200 hours per week" (Valiani 2011: 7).

Cutting back on nurses puts tremendous pressure on the delivery of health-care services. In 2010, in a troubling twist, doctors at a cash-strapped hospital in the Kootenays (B.C.) proposed paying nurses out of their own pockets to keep operating rooms running. Dr. Grant, an anesthesiologist, commented that, given the fee-for-service funding model, surgeons "would increase their revenues if they paid nurses to stay on staff" (Scallan 2010).

Undoubtedly, the changes in nursing work reflect neoliberal rationaliza- tion and work restructuring. The shifts have been described as deskilling or proletarianization (McPherson 1996) or "deprofessionalization" charac- terized by "a diminution of independence, increasing stratification and division of labour, and growing revolt against assembly-line conditions" (Stinson and Wagner, quoted in Mansell and Dodd 2005: 198). In a cogent example, more than seven hundred female nurses who work in the federal public service won a $150 million settlement in 2012. At the core of the successful human rights complaint was the fact that the "nurses were listed as administrative and clerical staff while working for the federal public ser- vice, instead of being classified as health professionals" (CBC News 2012).

PUBLIC SECTOR STRIKES, FEMINIZATION OF MILITANCY AND NURSES' STRIKES

Even though many public sector workers are deemed essential, denied the right to strike and often legislated back to work, an analysis of the Canadian stoppages data suggests the growing significance of public sector militancy in the landscape of labour relations conflict. Between 2000 and 2009, 27 percent of all stoppages (592) were in the public sector (the highest percentage in the last five decades). These stoppages involved more than 69 percent of all workers on strike.[7] The roots of this militancy are complex but certainly include the shift in union membership demographics toward the public sec- tor and the resistance by public sector workers to sustained attacks on the public sector, which have included wage freezes and rollbacks, downsizing, contracting out and privatization and assaults on public sector bargaining rights (Panitch and Swartz 2003).

Statistical data on the Canadian labour market reveals a significant trend toward the feminization of public sector militancy. Feminization speaks to demographic profiles: the feminization of work (more part-time, low-paid and often precarious jobs, employment patterns associated with women's work), the feminization of the workforce (increasing numbers of women workers), the feminization of union density (higher percentage of unionized women) and the concomitant feminization of union membership (a greater propor- tion of union members who are women) (Uppal 2011). These demographic transformations set the stage for the feminization of strikes, that is, those involved in strikes are more likely to be women. Although statistics are not available that demonstrate the exact proportion of women and men involved in any particular strike, the growth and increasing feminization of the public sector, especially in health and education, the importance of public sector workers to union density and the significance of strikes in this sector support the general claim for the feminization of strikes (Briskin 2007b).

In Canada, over 90 percent of RNs are women (Shields and Wilkins 2005: xii), the vast majority of whom work in the public sector. Health care is one of the most highly unionized sectors of the economy. Despite the historic resistance of nurses to unionization, nurses are more likely to be in unions than almost any other occupational group, in part because Canadian nurses' unions represent full-time, part-time and casual nurses. In 2010, 87 percent of nurses were unionized, higher than union density rates for the public sector overall (CFNU 2011: 1). Only teachers have a higher union coverage at 89 percent (Uppal 2011). The Canadian Federation of Nurses Unions is the eighth largest affiliate in the Canadian Labour Congress (CLC).[8]

Work stoppage data in Canada points to 106 public sector strikes by nurses' unions between 1960 and 2009, some of which were illegal and most of which garnered widespread popular support. During that time period, 163,872 Canadian nurses were on strike.[9] The three periods of nurses' strikes described in Table 1 coincide with health-care restructuring and cutbacks, the introduction of neoliberal health policy and government interventions into the collective bargaining process.

Table 3 Waves of Nurses' Strikes in Canada, 1960–2009

Years	Strikes	% of all nurses' strikes from 1960–2009	Number of nurses on strike
1980–82	17	16%	17,963
1985–91	43	40.5%	95,755
1998–99	14	13%	17,600
Total in three waves	74	69.5%	131,318
Total 1960–2009	106	100%	163,872

Source: Work Stoppage Data, Workplace Information Directorate, Human Resources and Social Development Canada.

Certainly in the 1980s, many strikes were in response to egregious government interventions in wage-setting (Palmer 1992: 359–60). Later strikes have focused not only on wages but also increasingly on work restructuring and its impact on stress, working conditions and the ability of nurses to deliver quality care.[10]

Evidence also suggests that government austerity measures have gender-specific intent and impact, given their consistent and heavy-handed attacks on the public sector and the rights of workers to strike. As Darcy and Lauzon (1983: 172–3) point out, "the right to strike is a women's issue [given] the fact that organized working women are heavily concentrated in the public sector, where anti-strike legislation is directed." Armstrong (2012: 8) also drew this link: "Attacks on unions in the public sector are attacks on women who make up the majority of unionized workers there." Nurse militancy takes up the implications of such attacks. For example, in discussing the Saskatchewan nurses' strike, Debra McPherson, secretary-treasurer of the National Federation of Nurses' Unions, argued that

> The government [has] failed to take into account that most nurses are middle-aged women who have plenty of life experience and aren't easily cowed ... If Mr. Romanow [premier of Saskatchewan's NDP government] thinks these 8,000 women are going to back down, he had just better take his testosterone hissy fit and stuff it. (Debra McPherson quoted in Parker 1999)

In her view, the resentment stemmed from the fact that governments everywhere have shown no reluctance to cut or freeze the wages of public sector employees, most of whom are women. "The public sector is constantly the brunt of wage restraint ... But if they think they can keep women working for less, they are going to have to think again. We're past that" (ibid.).

THE PUBLIC INTEREST AND THE POLITICIZATION OF CARING

Public sector strikes regularly adopt a discursive frame focused on the public interest: "Public workers' movements are constrained to frame their claims as 'public needs' ... turning bargaining into a political debate over public policy" (Johnston 1994: 12). The struggles of nurses certainly support this argument. Following strikes in 1988 and 1991, Saskatchewan nurses defied back-to-work legislation for ten days in 1999 and framed their defiance in terms of the public interest. Speaking to the convention of the Canadian Labour Congress, nurse Nancy Syles reported:

> There were nurses on the picket line who told me, "I've never even had a speeding ticket." But you know they never flinched. They were willing to stay on that picket line and maybe even be sent to jail ... All we want to do as nurses is to deliver safe, excellent nursing care ... We cannot do this in the working conditions we have now. (Mickleburgh 1999)

In a letter to the editor of the *Regina Leader-Post*, Laurie Swift (1999), a nurse in Regina, wrote:

> This issue is really about the nursing shortage which … has led to horrific and unsafe working conditions and compromised patient care … We are taking a stand for the people of Saskatchewan: you, me, our families, our communities, as the caregivers and patient advocates that we are.

However, nurses' employers and the state (which funds health care) also have a vested interest in mobilizing the discourse of the public interest. Haiven (1991: 8) points out that, in seeking legitimacy, the state attempts to exercise "a monopoly in defining and protecting the … 'public interest.'" He speaks of the "wrestling match over possession of stewardship of the public interest" and notes that "in every nurses' strike to date, the question of ownership of the 'public interest' has been hotly contested." In fact, Gindin and Hurley (2010: 2) point to the ways government traps, marginalizes and isolates public sector workers by "cynically set[ting] itself up as the defender of services … [I]f workers demand improved compensation, this would only prove that they didn't care about the public."

At the same time, in its promotion of individual rather than community responsibility, neoliberal radical individualism has undermined the discourse of the public good. This invocation of individualism highlights the discursive and ideological shift from state to family and individual, exposes essentialist assumptions about women's apparently natural responsibility for caring and has fuelled nurse resistance.

Undoubtedly, the fact that nurses do caring work largely located in the public sector is significant to their consciousness, tactics and strategy, the political discourses they employ and the impact of their strikes. Historically, many women who serve client groups are ambivalent about making demands around wages and working conditions and engaging in public protest. In fact, women's responsibility for caring work has been actively mobilized to deter women from striking:

> Women are trained to feel responsible for the people they care for, whether at home or on the job. Consequently, they can easily be made to feel guilty if they refuse to take care … And when they do strike, the media may depict them as "heartless and unfeeling." (Darcy and Lauzon 1983: 175)

All international accounts of nurses' strike activity allude to the conflict between striking and caring (Brown et al. 2006: 206).

However, this research suggests that increasingly nurses' dedication to caring work may encourage rather than prevent them from going on strike. The question has become "not whether that action is ethical but whether it is unethical not to take action" (Jennings and Western 1997: 281). In addressing this dilemma, McKeown, Stowell-Smith and Foley (1999: 146) note that "the understanding of industrial action [has moved] into the discursive domain of compassion and care, stressing the symbiosis of industrial action with concern for patient welfare: declaring militancy as professionally desirable." In their study of the 1999 Irish nurses' strike, Brown et al. (2006: 205) confirm that "the act of striking itself is an act of advocacy."

Nurses have confronted health-care restructuring, nursing shortages, intensification of work, precarious employment and gendered hierarchies with a militant discourse around the public interest and a reconstitution and reclamation of caring, what I call "the politicization of caring." Traditionally, caring and professionalism were seen in opposition to one another: the first based on narrow, essentialist and gendered expectations, a paradigm increasingly rejected by nurses; and the second based on technical expertise and often embraced by nurses to further their claims for professional recognition. The politicization of caring rejects essentialist assumptions as well as the "sentimentalization of caring" (Nelson and Gordon 2006), the individualistic moral imperative to care and the separation of caring and expertise. It acknowledges caring as a form of expertise and revalues the expertise of nurses. It recognizes the broad political and social implications of the caring paradigm and the social responsibilities attendant on it. It moves the discourse of caring into the collective and political-economic realm.

Such an approach is also evident in the United States. On June 10, 2010, for example, 12,000 Minnesota nurses went on a coordinated twenty-four hour strike across fourteen hospitals to demand strict nurse-patient ratios: "To walk for patients" (Mador 2010). Rachleff (2010) noted that the Minnesota Nurses Association (MNA) challenged management prerogatives.

> Nurses are claiming the right to a voice in how their labor is used, and they are seeking clear numbers and explicit contract language to protect that voice ... MNA ... has pursued this agenda in order to put patients before profits, thereby improving the quality of care. In doing so, they have sought to connect the nurses with the very people — patients, prospective patients, the families of patients — who are dependent upon the quality of that service, that professional care.

Between 2010 and 2012, Californian nurses have gone on strike more than eight times. Winslow (2011) commented:

> It is difficult to exaggerate the significance of these strikes. In the face of a deafening chorus preaching austerity, of the near universal demand — from corporations to politicians — for concessions,

these workers have said no. ... [T]hese workers are resisting cuts in staffing and the implicit demand that they abandon their role as patients' advocates.

Speaking about the National Health Service in the U.K., Thornley explains: "The public understand [*sic*] ... that poor pay and conditions impact directly on the quality of patient care. In defending their own interests through industrial action and strike action, history has shown nurses are also safeguarding the public interest" (quoted in Jennings and Western 1997: 281). In reference to the illegal nurses' strike in 1988, Edmonton Working Women (Canada) commented:

> The country's attention was captured by the courage, strength and unity of the members of the United Nurses of Alberta who went on an illegal strike. They defied the law to defend their own democratic rights and to oppose the erosion of workers' rights on all fronts ... [and to] fight for the patients' rights to quality, publicly funded health care. (quoted in Coulter 1993: 56)

The widespread mobilization of nurses and the discourses that frame this militancy support a claim for the politicization of caring, that is, a recognition of the collective responsibility for caring, and the impact of deteriorating conditions of nursing work on quality care; the rejection of essentialist claims that women are responsible for caring work by virtue of being women; the demand that the skills involved in caring work be recognized and rewarded; and the willingness to mobilize collectively to these ends.

THE PUBLIC TRUST

As part of the adoption of a discursive frame focused on the public interest, striking public sector workers frequently try to mobilize community and coalitional support. In fact, Peirce (2003: 273) makes the point that "public sector unionism is inherently political, with efforts directed towards winning and maintaining public support both for public sector unions' specific rights and for the government spending that under girds the services public sector workers provide."

Many Canadian nurses' strikes have been characterized by strong popular support and by active involvement of other unions, the community, the public, women's organizations and other progressive movements. In many countries where nurses have gone on strike, heightened attention has been paid to the event, and opinion polls have tracked public response. And despite the inconvenience such strikes cause, support for nurses and trust ratings have been surprisingly strong.

In fact, despite fourteen high-profile nurses' strikes in Canada in 1998 and 1999, a 2000 poll gave nurses the highest trust rating of any profession (O'Brien 2002: 28). In a 2007 survey on trustworthy professions, nurses ranked at 87 percent (second only to firefighters at 93 percent), despite the fact that labour unions ranked at only 19 percent (Ipsos Reid 2007).[11] A 2009 poll found that three out of four Canadians would choose increasing the number of nurses over a tax cut. The majority also opposed government increasing the number of patients nurses must care for (CFNU/Nanos Research 2009).

And even when nurses went on strike illegally or broke the law in other ways, public support has remained resilient and sometimes even passionate. The lengthy illegal strike by Québec nurses in 1999 garnered massive support from the public, 72 percent of whom thought the nurses' wage demands reasonable (Peritz 1999).

> Unable to bring the nurses to heel with the existing legislation, the Parti Québécois government … removed the right to strike entirely and upped the penalties. But union members continued their walkout, to an outpouring of public sympathy, including polls showing majority public support and 120,000 signatures on a petition. (Haiven and Haiven 2002: 7)

In a 2001 protest in Nova Scotia,

> Two hundred nurses were defying the government and breaking the law. They were sitting in the middle of the busiest Halifax intersection. Traffic was backed up for blocks. The bus driver at the head of the jam wasn't moving: "I'm in a union too," he said. No passengers complained. The folks on the sidewalks cheered. The cops just stood back and watched. (Hambling 2002: 12)

Punitive measures by governments have often increased public support for nurses. For example, when more than 11,000 staff nurses in Alberta went on illegal strike for nineteen days in 1988, public support for nurses increased concomitantly with punitive measures against the nurses (Haiven 1991: 14; Coulter 1993). And many strike narratives specifically point to the strength of public support as critical to the success of the strike. For example, a 1988 strike in Saskatchewan received extensive public support, and speculation suggested that this support prevented government intervention (Haiven 1991: 17). A study of media and public opinion on the Finnish nurses' struggle (based on the mass resignation of 16,000 nurses in 2007) concluded:

> In taking extreme industrial action to fight for their working conditions, nurses are positioned as going over and beyond their duties by risking their own employment for the development of the healthcare

sector at large … [N]urses are positioned as heroic reformers serving the interests of citizens. (Henttonen et al. 2011: 13)

Furthermore, unlike the widespread attacks on public sector wages, support for paying nurses a fair wage is noteworthy.[12] During the 2001 Nova Scotia nurses' struggle, Ipsos Reid found that

> 78 percent of Nova Scotians said that the nurses were being more fair and reasonable than the government. 86 percent opposed forced overtime. 73 percent said nurses were not paid enough … More than six in ten said that they would rather boost nurses' pay and benefits than have the government's promised tax cut. (O'Brien 2002: 25)

In the discursive struggle between the state and the nurses over advocacy of the public interest, evidence of public support for and public trust in nurses suggests that they have been quite successful advocates. They do not seem to face the barrage of criticism and resentment with which other components of the public sector have had to contend, especially around wage claims.

CONCLUSION

This chapter has explored the emergence of a militant discourse among nurses focused on the public interest, what I have called the politicization of caring, which has supported a new approach to the ethics of striking and has created the conditions for widespread public support for nurses' strikes. It also suggests that public sector strikes have the potential to renew unions, build community support for public services and challenge legislative and employer attacks on collective bargaining.

Nurse militancy also offers a paradigm that supports the expansion rather than the narrowing of the collective bargaining agenda. Gindin and Hurley (2010: 5–6) point to government attempts to narrow the scope of collective bargaining, often by removing "wages and benefit improvements from negotiations." They call for unions to respond by "expanding collective bargaining": "What if public sector unions refused to settle collective agreements unless the settlements address the level, quality and administration of the services being provided?" This chapter points to the fact that, in Canada, striking nurses have resisted austerity initiatives in precisely this way, calling for the expansion of the collective bargaining agenda to take more account of patient care, to defend their rights to advocate for patients and to protect the quality of health care.

Key to the success of nurse militancy may well be defending public services not only during periods of collective bargaining but continuously. Noteworthy is the campaign for a financial transaction tax (FTT), sometimes called the Robin Hood Tax, by National Nurses United (NNU), the largest union of registered nurses in the United States (Gaus 2011). This campaign is part of what the NNU calls "a main street contract for the American people," which seeks to counter the corporate agenda with union and community demands for job creation, guaranteed health care, secure retirements and decent education. "We see a better world is possible, and we know how to pay for it. Our way as patient advocates, as engaged community members, as global citizens is clear: organize, organize, organize" (NNU n.d.).

Nurse militancy is also part of a long tradition of union women's organizing and resistance, and evidence in this chapter suggests it offers potential to defend public services and protect workers' rights. This is a significant contribution in the current austerity conjuncture, in which public sector workers are targeted, and communities are under considerable attack from privatization and public-private partnerships, deep cuts to social services and health care and the invocation of individual responsibility and the concomitant muting, if not elimination, of the concept of "the public good" (Martinez and García 2000). Finally, nurse militancy not only challenges the association of militancy with men but also the marginalization and increasing criminalization of protest. In its capacity to build public support, nurse militancy helps to mainstream and legitimize militancy itself.

Notes

1. I would like to thank Rachel Hurst for her work in the newspaper archives and Kristine Klement, whose work on the HRSDC data has been invaluable. This research was partly funded by the Social Sciences and Humanities Research Council of Canada (SSHRC) and the Faculty of Arts at York University.
2. This chapter draws freely on Briskin 2011c, 2012 and 2013.
3. In many countries, the relationship between professional nurses' associations and unions of nurses is a tangled, uneasy and complex one. A simplified narrative is as follows. For many decades, professional nurses' associations were vehemently opposed to strikes, both to protect their claims to professional status and to underscore their commitments to care and service. However, deteriorating conditions for nurses led professional associations to adopt various ways of bargaining collectively, often short of certifying as unions. This seen-to-be gentler and more professional approach, untainted by the image of working-class, blue collar and industrial unions of men, was largely unsuccessful, and nurses began to organize into unions.
4. National Health Expenditure Trends Data Tables, Table B.4.5, Canadian Institute of Health Information. <secure.cihi.ca/estore/productFamily. htm?locale=en&pf=PFC1671>.
5. Noteworthy is the extent to which hospitals in the global north rely on international nurse migration. See Valiani 2012.
6. National Health Expenditure Trends Data Tables, Data Table B RN1, Canadian Institute of Health Information. <cihi.ca/cihi-ext-portal/internet/

en/document/spending+and+health+workforce/workforce/nurses/stats_nursing_2009>.

7. The author has negotiated full access to the records of each Canadian stoppage from 1946–2009.

8. The CFNU includes eight provincial nurses' unions (excluding British Columbia and Québec) and has, in total, 136,000 members (CFNU n.d.).

9. Identifying strikes by nurses in the data is not straightforward. First, the data focuses on strikes and not strikers. Strike data can be disaggregated by industry but not by occupational categories, so it is not possible to capture nurses on strikes through occupational sorting. Second, although the data can be sorted by union and most nurses are in unions of nurses, others are in health-care or public sector unions of which they are only one part. The data does not present a full picture of all nurses who have gone on strike in Canada.

10. Militant strikes by nurses are not only a Canadian phenomenon. In the last three decades, nurses have gone on strike in many countries including the U.K., the U.S., Australia, Japan, New Zealand, Israel, Ireland, Denmark, Sweden, Poland, Portugal, Kenya, Fiji, India and South Africa. Nurses have also used innovative nonstrike tactics of resistance such as mass resignations, most successfully in Finland in 2007 (Briskin 2012) but also in Canada as early as 1950, in 1969 in New Brunswick and in 2001 in Nova Scotia.

11. The 2007 poll was conducted for Sympatico/MSN by Ipsos Reid. In a 2012 poll that asked Canadians if they think the gains made by unions benefit everyone, only 46 percent agreed, an ongoing dilemma for all public sector unions (Ballantyne and Staples 2012).

12. A 2012 poll in British Columbia found considerable support for job action by public sector workers in support of a cost of living increase. The poll showed that the majority of B.C. residents agreed with the statement that public sector workers should at least get a cost of living increase without having to take cuts elsewhere in their collective agreement (38 percent strongly agree, 36 percent somewhat agree). The majority of people (61 percent) also appeared to back the public sector workers' job action and one-day strike (BCFL 2012).

8. CLASSROOM STRUGGLE

Teachers' Unions, Collective Bargaining and Neoliberal Education Reform

Andy Hanson

Public education remains a significant cost to the public purse, but it is necessary for the functioning of capitalist democracy. The linkages between education, capitalist enterprise and the state have long pitted teachers against tax-averse capitalists, politicians and their supporters. Since the 1970s, teachers have also been central in resisting neoliberal state policy in Canada, because education itself has been a key target of neoliberal restructuring. This chapter argues that while provincial responsibility for education has fragmented teachers' activism, teachers' unions have nonetheless found common means to resist governments intent on reducing the public sector and rolling back past gains. By defending their working conditions, teachers focus attention on education quality and funding and mobilize segments of the public against retrenchment policies.

In Canada, education falls under provincial jurisdiction. As a result, teachers are subject to thirteen provincial and territorial labour regimes and organized by even more unions, each of which achieved collective bargaining rights at different times between 1941 and 1989 (Williams-Whitt 2012: 130; Yukon 1989). However, all teachers have had to engage in collective struggles to win the rights to collectively bargain and (in some places) to strike, despite strong and continuing pressures to restrict such rights.

Such opposition is confounding given that teachers' collective bargaining rights have had little direct influence on the structure, form and content of education systems. Provincial/territorial education acts establish the "bricks and mortar" design of schools, their contents and location, what courses are offered, which bodies have decision-making authority and funding structures (Nova Scotia 2009; Ontario 1990). However, unions *have* influenced class sizes, the time available to teachers for marking and preparing lessons, wages and benefits that attract qualified teachers, health and safety conditions, teachers' workload and the relationship between teachers, administrators and trustees. Except for wages and benefits, these issues — teachers' working conditions — are the same conditions under which students learn, improvements to which help both teachers and students (Leithwood 2006: 5, 89). Such an appeal also resonates with parents. During the 1997 two-week, province-wide teachers' strike in Ontario, an Angus Reid poll commissioned by the *Toronto Sun* demonstrated that 59 percent of parents supported the teachers who launched the political strike in an effort to resist the Conservative government's restructuring of the education sector (Walkom 1997). Public support for teachers stems from the location of their reproductive labour,[1] which gives teachers authority at the classroom door, thereby opening a sympathetic space for their grievances to be heard when they enter the public arena. At the same time, teachers' position as caregivers of children arouses public censure when unions call upon their members to vacate their classrooms. The continued decline in union density also threatens to erode public support for the benefit to teachers of union activity.

THE CONTRADICTORY ROLE OF PUBLIC EDUCATION: STATE-CAPITALISM LINKAGES

The public education project in Canada has always been contradictory in its purposes. For its originators, it was a twofold process meant to produce worker-citizens disciplined to the rigours of the modern workplace and the rituals of British citizenship (Prentice 1977: 17–18). Capitalist relationships continue to govern the public education project. Employers rely on public institutions to structure labour markets (by producing differently "qualified" workers) and to train workers to accept the hegemony of capitalist economic relations (Sears 2003: 78–82). At the same time, they pressure governments to minimize the taxes that pay for education in order to maximize profits generated by capitalist activity. Furthermore, citizenship training makes students aware of civil, political and social rights — tools that can be used to undermine the dominance of the marketplace (Marshall 2009: 148–54). The socialization of children and enabling the mode of production are interconnected elements of social reproduction contained in schooling (Luxton 2006: 27). Parents will go to great lengths to secure an education for their children with the understanding that to be uneducated in the twenty-first century severely limits life chances in an increasingly competitive job market, while the school's responsibility for child care frees women from constant domestic obligations and permits them to engage in waged labour.

As a contradictory and gendered form of reproductive labour, education produces important tensions in the relationships between teachers, the state, the wider labour movement and the broader public. The fetishization of academic qualifications, the feminization of elementary teaching and the attachment of teachers to their professional status all have roots in the gendered stratification of education. In the nineteenth century, the state pursued the professionalization of education so as to discipline teachers to the standardization of citizenship and skills training by requiring qualifications in pedagogy and curricula from state training facilities (Prentice 1977: 17). When teachers began to negotiate collectively, they appropriated professionalism in order to enter labour relations as skilled workers with greater bargaining power than was typical of other feminized occupations (Ozga and Lawn 1981: v–x; Warburton 1986: 213). A pervasive effect of teachers' efforts to win privilege by attaching to professional status has been to distance teachers from other workers (Green 2008: 155).

Teachers navigate these contradictions in their daily work and their forms of collective action. They discipline their students through the routines of the school day but also encourage their full development as people. They have achieved a degree of control over their work lives through union-based collective action but also remain agents of the state (and capital). Because of their position at the nexus between worker training, socialization of norms of citizenship and human development, teachers have always been of particular concern to political and economic elites, as reflected in the various forms of legislation meant to govern their behaviour and power.

LEGISLATING EDUCATION:
FROM THE PUBLIC EDUCATION PROJECT TO COLLECTIVE BARGAINING

Current provincial legislation governing education falls into four categories: governance and credentials; recognition of teachers' unions; the right to collective bargaining; and reversing the gains made by teachers. Each of these categories of regulation characterizes a period in labour relations in the education sector, but all reflect attempts to shape and contain the power of teachers.

Before Confederation, colonial jurisdictions legislated school acts, establishing governance structures and teachers' qualifications. The establishment of Normal Schools as state training facilities standardized entrance requirements, pedagogy and curriculum and established a top-down governance model as an arm of the British state (Hanson 2009: 118–20). Nova Scotia passed its first *Education Act* in 1808 (NSSBA 2012), and Ontario, then Canada West, passed the *Common School Act* in 1846 (Graham 1974: 171). At the time of Confederation, each province and territory retained responsibility for its school system and the legislation concerning education. This was particularly important to Québécois francophones seeking protections for their language and culture.

Conditions in nineteenth-century teaching included overcrowded classrooms, low pay and exploitative working conditions, particularly for women

(Prentice 1985: 97–121). In the latter half of the nineteenth century, teachers in Québec and the Maritimes began to organize to represent their interests to trustees (QPAT 2012; NSTU n.d.). Teachers' conflated identity as members of both professional organizations and unions undermined expressions of militancy. Moreover, provincial authority for both education and labour resulted in a very uneven front for teachers' unionization.

Immediately after the First World War, new teachers' unions were organized across Canada.[2] They focused on improving conditions in schools, teachers' wages and pensions. In the 1920s in Québec and the western provinces, the unions mounted the first teacher strikes (CTF 1992). By the end of the Second World War, teachers' unions representing most of the teachers in their province had been part of the education landscape for two decades. However, in the mid to late 1940s, amid important changes in Canada's labour relations framework that provided legal support for collective bargaining, provinces enacted a second category of education legislation to further regulate labour relations between teachers and trustees. The new legislation granted teachers' unions closed shop status and dues check-off, ensuring their continued existence through statutory designation, but the new regime importantly denied them collective bargaining rights (Schucher and Slinn 2012: 22–25).[3]

The late 1960s, however, saw an upsurge in public sector workers' organizing and militancy. Those who had been excluded from the postwar labour relations legislation, including teachers, began to fight for collective bargaining rights, primarily through the use of illegal strikes (Heron 2012: 94–98). Between 1966 and 1967, with their militancy given ideological support by the Quiet Revolution, nearly seventeen thousand Québécois teachers were on strike (LeBlanc 1974; Canadian Teachers' Federation 1992). Newfoundland teachers walked out for over a month in 1971 demanding — and winning — the right to strike (NLTA n.d.). In Ontario, a one-day province-wide strike in December 1973 gained teachers the right to strike (Richter 2008: 37). British Columbia's teachers developed their strategies during the 1970s and '80s under premiers Vander Zalm and Bennett and marched in the 1983 general strike, Operation Solidarity, for the right to strike, among other issues, a goal finally achieved in 1987 (BCTF n.d.). In the face of such militancy, the state was forced into a third category of legislation, and by the end of the 1980s, teachers had won the right to collective bargaining, albeit under labour regimes unique to the education sector and not always with the right to strike. By 1990, teachers across the country had improved their salaries and benefits, established seniority rights and were negotiating their working conditions.

However, the unique legislation granting collective bargaining rights to teachers introduced additional steps in the process beyond those required in the provincial/territorial labour relations acts, putting limitations on the unions while still granting their demand for collective bargaining. For example, New Brunswick teachers were required to vote on the school board's final offer before they could strike (New Brunswick 1973: s. 77). The Ontario legislation established the Education Relations Commission to oversee teachers' collective bargaining (Ontario 1975: s. 59–62). In Manitoba[4] and Prince Edward Island,[5] teachers could bargain but not strike; binding arbitration remained the dispute resolution mechanism (MTS 2012; PEITF 2012). New Brunswick, Québec,[6] Northwest Territories (Northwest Territories 1996) and Nunavut (Nunavut 2011) included teachers in legislation that applied to all public sector workers. Each of the teachers' unions has developed strategic responses that work within the labour regime unique to its jurisdiction.

WHO NEGOTIATES: PROVINCIAL AND LOCAL NEGOTIATIONS

In all provinces and territories, legislation requires teachers to negotiate with local boards of education, the state or some combination of the two (Québec 2012; Ontario 1997). Over the past half century, education funding has been almost entirely removed from local property taxes and become drawn from the general revenues of provincial/territorial governments.[7] Without the right to tax, boards of education have lost their economic authority, and labour negotiations have tended to migrate to the provincial level.

Pressure for province-wide bargaining has been one strategy applied by governments in an effort to contain the economic demands of teachers. In Saskatchewan, government appointees outnumber trustees on the collective bargaining committee (Saskatchewan 2010: s. 237). In Alberta, the Minister of Education and the president of the Alberta School Boards Association are the employer's negotiating team.[8] In Newfoundland and Labrador, the School Board Committee's chief negotiator is an appointee of the Treasury Board, which has "sole and final decision on the tentative rejection or approval of a proposal" during negotiations (Newfoundland and Labrador 2007: s. 10).

The majority of the provinces and territories have some form of province-wide bargaining, often in conjunction with local bargaining. Four of the smallest jurisdictions, Prince Edward Island,[9] New Brunswick,[10] the Yukon[11] and Nunavut (NTA 2005), negotiate a single collective agreement for all teachers with no local negotiations taking place. The Newfoundland and Labrador Teachers' Association negotiates one collective agreement for Newfoundland and one for Labrador (NLTA 2012: 7). The Northwest Territories Teachers' Association negotiates two collective agreements, one for teachers in Yellowknife and one for the rest of the territory.[12]

The legislation in Manitoba, Ontario and Alberta grants bargaining authority to the locals in principle. Historically, school boards had the authority to levy taxes to enrich the provincial grants they received for education. However, as provincial budgets came to embrace neoliberal imperatives, demonizing social services and the taxes that support them, the Ontario and Alberta governments sought ways to restrict the scope of local bargaining and removed the power of trustees to tax. Manitoba is the only province that still retains entirely local negotiations.[13] Locals conduct negotiations with representatives of the boards of education while the central office of the Manitoba Teachers' Society provides support. If the two sides reach an impasse, binding arbitration is applied and collective bargaining ends. Since Manitoba teachers have no way to enforce their demands, the state retains control of wages and working conditions.

Until 1998, the locals of the five teachers' unions in Ontario, like those in Manitoba, had the authority to negotiate with their boards and sign final agreements. If the two sides reached an impasse, locals could strike and the union would provide strike pay and other support. In 1998, the Conservative government repealed the former legislation governing teachers' labour relations, placed them under the *Ontario Labour Relations Act* (OLRA) and removed the ability of trustees to levy taxes (Ontario 1997). Although locals still conducted negotiations, the OLRA established the central unions as the final authority during teachers' collective bargaining. The change paved the way for experiments in two-tiered bargaining in Ontario.

Nova Scotia, Québec, Saskatchewan[14] and British Columbia have two-tiered bargaining regimes. With Ontario and Alberta moving in that direction, this has become the most common teacher bargaining regime in Canada; cost items are decided provincially and organizational matters locally. The diversity of Canadian labour practices in education developed in response to the dialectics of the teacher-state relationship. Teachers have had to work within the legislative framework of their particular jurisdiction. A single bargaining unit has fostered greater union strength in British Columbia, but it has done little to develop militancy in Manitoba or Prince Edward Island. Also, a distinction must be made between one union representing all the teachers in a province/territory as they negotiate with boards of education and centralized bargaining where unions must negotiate directly with the state. Governments that have chosen to become involved in the bargaining process have generally done so to advance their neoliberal ideological goals, which have also informed their legislative approach to teacher unions over the past thirty years.

LEGISLATION TO REVERSE TEACHERS' GAINS: REFORM AND RETRENCHMENT

The years between 1975 and 2013 constitute a critical period of regime change in Canada. The transnational neoliberal project was taken up by economic and political elites so as to dismantle the Keynesian state and with it the postwar social accord. The legal protections that had sanctioned union activity were undermined through the application of new forms of legislation (Panitch and Swartz 1993: 80–85, 102 and this volume). In 1975, Prime Minister Trudeau introduced neoliberalism into Canada with the first round of wage and price controls. Legislated wage controls would continue for a decade, signalling the beginning of retrenchment and the neoliberal reform of state institutions.

As the nexus of institutionalized worker-citizen training and its labour market outcomes, teachers were an early target of the neoliberal project (Sears 2003: 59–83). The cost borne by society for the education of its children came under close scrutiny and resulted in pressure for the commodification and deprofessionalization of teaching. Although elites continued to value education (of a sort) as a source of competitiveness in globalized markets, the resources available for public education were substantially reduced. Ontario alone took $2 billion out of its education budget under the Harris government (Mackenzie 2002). Increasing teachers' workload and restraining their wage increases promised to deliver smaller education budgets while leaving education's social reproductive role intact.

Neoliberal governments have thus used legislation to restrict teachers' rights to bargain. Since 1990, provincial governments of all political stripes have attacked teachers' collective agreements and restricted collective bargaining. In 1993 in Ontario, the NDP government mandated unpaid holidays. The Conservative government that followed rolled back teachers' working conditions and engaged in a concerted campaign of teacher bashing (Sears 2003: 234–9). Nova Scotia teachers fought against a two-year wage freeze forced on them by the Liberal government in 1996 (Forbes 1996). Under consecutive Conservative governments, Alberta reduced its spending on education to tenth in the country as a percentage of GDP by cutting programs, thereby increasing teachers' workload and placing demands on students and parents to equip schools through fundraising (Soucek and Pannu 1996: 52–54, 61–62). In 2002 and again in 2004, the B.C. Liberal government legislated working conditions out of the collective bargaining process and imposed a contract that resulted in two thousand teachers losing their jobs.[15]

Provincial/territorial governments have also pressured teachers into new collective bargaining practices without changing the legislation that governs negotiations. Ontario, Alberta and to some degree British Columbia have moved teachers' collective bargaining under the labour relations acts where governments can swiftly enact legislation to suppress labour militancy. Since 2000, collective bargaining has become meaningless in British Columbia as the Liberal government repeatedly legislated the terms of collective agreements (BCTF n.d.). In 2008, the Ontario Liberal government forced provincial negotiations on the teachers' unions for all items that had costs attached (Ontario Ministry of Education 2009). Recently, Alberta's teachers were forced into negotiating a "tripartite agreement" with the Minister of Education and the Alberta School Boards Association (ATA 2012). These examples of governments imposing provincial negotiations on teachers reflect a tendency of neoliberal governments to centralize power structures to control the bargaining process. State actors have learned that the most effective weapon against the legal rights of workers is new legislation that undermines long-held entitlements. Governments, supported by right-wing think tanks, have reshaped hegemonic assumptions concerning the role of the state in providing public services.

UNION ACTIVISM: MAKING GAINS IN NEOLIBERAL TIMES

Like other public sector workers, teachers and their unions have mobilized to resist legislated assaults on wages, working conditions, job security and the right to collective bargaining. As they did during the struggle to establish collective bargaining rights, teachers have used militant tactics to defend the gains they won through free collective bargaining. Across the country, and despite important variations in legislation, bargaining structures and teacher unions' orientations, province-wide teachers' strikes have been a common response to the effects of funding cuts to education (Canadian Teachers' Federation 1992).

In 1980, 73,000 Québec teachers struck for two weeks to protect previously negotiated class size restrictions but were legislated back to work. In 1982, Québec teachers were out of their classrooms again, this time for one day in opposition to wage cuts and increased workload. A year later they staged a thirteen-day province-wide strike to protest wage rollbacks and workload increases (ibid.). In 2011, the Centrale des syndicats du Québec (CSQ) threatened to strike over the Québec government's plan to cut school board budgets in half (CBC News 2011b).

In the Atlantic provinces, Newfoundland and Labrador teachers walked out to protest their working conditions for fourteen days in 1984 and thirty-two days in 1986 (Canadian Teachers' Federation 1992). In New Brunswick, teachers engaged in a forty-day work-to-rule campaign in 1981 to protect class size and imposed the same sanctions again in 1989 over wages and working conditions.[16] Nova Scotia teachers voted to strike to retain their collective bargaining rights in 1995 (Forbes 1996: 121).

On the Prairies, Alberta teachers confronted the Klein government with a strike in 2002 (Barnetson 2010). Despite the government's use of back-to-work legislation, the strike ended with wage and pension improvements. In Saskatchewan, teachers held their first province-wide strike in May 2011 as a response to the Saskatchewan Party capping teachers' wages (CBC News 2011c).

In British Columbia, 90 percent of teachers defied court injunctions and remained on picket lines in 1983 when the government threatened to remove seniority provisions (Canadian Teachers' Federation 1992). B.C. teachers held a one-day strike in 1987 to protest the changes to labour relations legislation. In 2011, they started the school year working to rule while they waited for a Supreme Court ruling on previous legislation (CBC News 2011d).

All five Ontario teachers' unions struck for two weeks in 1997 when the government changed the labour relations regime and threatened to degrade existing working conditions (Gidney 1999: 247–9). More recently, in 2012, Ontario's Bill 115, the *Putting Students First Act*, stripped entitlements from teachers' collective agreements, banned strikes and legislated the conditions of future bargaining. Teachers in the public system responded with a work-to-rule, rotating strikes and a court challenge (CBC News 2013).[17]

Province-wide strikes and job actions have not been the only response of teachers. When trustees became emboldened by neoliberal rhetoric, teacher locals responded with workplace sanctions. Although locals are smaller in size, the strength of these strikes is noteworthy. In 1990, teachers in Regina went on strike for 111 days to demand improvements in their working conditions. Their efforts gained them long-sought guaranteed preparation time. In 1992 in Alberta, ten thousand teachers in ten different boards went on strike to resist trustees imposing management-rights clauses and won improvements in wages and benefits. In 2001, Yukon teachers held a series of rotating strikes to protest a legislated contract that reduced wages.

Under threat of heavy fines for individual teachers and their unions, decertification or back-to-work legislation, teachers' unions have had to tread carefully, given that the provinces that fund their employers hold all the legislative power (Barnetson 2010: 12). Yet they have been willing to place themselves on the public stage to directly challenge neoliberal policy and were able to make gains when governments offered concessions to avoid politically volatile labour disputes.

Three decades of neoliberalism have forced teachers' unions to mobilize in order to resist the depredations of austerity measures. The size of their membership ensures that they have an impact: they are amongst the largest labour organizations in the country. Since militancy pits them against the state, teachers' unions have had to operate on the workplace and political terrain simultaneously. The state's ability to pass punitive legislation has driven teachers to align their concerns with parents and other public interest groups to bring pressure to bear on political decision-makers. Teachers' claim that their interests align with those of students is weakest at the point of salary, benefits and pensions. Nonetheless, whenever governments reduce spending on education, students and teachers are mutually affected. While the unions have been able to capitalize on the stated intent behind retrenchment policies in order to enlarge their support, the success of teachers' unions and the improvements in standard of living that come with effective union activity has alienated segments of the working class, particularly those who are not unionized. Although they have become involved in labour's campaigns in some provinces, only a few teachers' unions have joined the Canadian Labour Congress and thus created institutional alliances with the broader labour movement.

CONCLUSION

While the division of constitutional authority over education and labour policy in Canada and the resulting fragmentation of teachers' unions isolate teachers and their unions geographically, nevertheless, when viewed from a national level, it becomes apparent that teachers' unions have adapted their strategies to align with general trends. In the 1960s and '70s, most teachers across Canada fought for the right to bargain and strike. In the 1980s and '90s, teachers' unions resisted concession bargaining, wage freezes and the ascent of neoliberalism. As governments began to use legislative means to attack teachers and their unions, teachers responded by joining the campaigns of other labour organizations and mounting substantial resistance of their own. In the new millennium, governments have become even more repressive as they attempt to entirely deny teachers collective bargaining rights. Although teachers' unions continue to come under attack, teachers' labour remains necessary for a disciplined workforce. The social position of teachers in reproductive labour ensures the unions of their membership base. As a result of their numbers and their proximity to the state, teachers have assumed a key role in challenging neoliberal governments.

Labour laws that were allegedly intended to establish a balance of power in the private sector have not translated well for public sector unions. Neoliberal state policy has required teachers' unions to confront governments through the courts and through militant expressions of union strength to ensure their own survival and to preserve space for collective bargaining. Political activism has become a requirement for teachers' unions that want to retain their right to negotiate with their employers. Union mobilization in response to government efforts to suppress collective bargaining challenges the legitimacy of neoliberal policies on the public stage while developing fluency in counter-hegemonic rhetoric within the rank and file. In order to protect past gains and achieve improvements, teachers' unions have had to develop a strategic politics of resistance superimposed on the collective bargaining process.

Notes

1. Social reproduction is work that ensures the continuation of the social structure, including the reproduction of the labour force through education and training (Braedley 2006: 216).
2. The earliest date of formation of teachers' unions according to their respective

websites are: QC 1864; PEI, 1880; NF, 1890; NS, 1895; AB, 1917; ON, 1918; MB, 1919; BC, 1919; SK, 1933; NB, 1946; NWT, 1953; YK, 1955; NU, 1999.

3. Examples of legislation recognizing union representation include the *Teachers Association Act* (Newfoundland); the *Teaching Profession Act* (Nova Scotia); the *Teaching Profession Act* (Ontario); the *Teachers' Federation Act* (Saskatchewan); and the *Teaching Profession Act* (Alberta).
4. Manitoba teachers were granted the right to strike in 1948 but lost it in 1956 (Britton 2006: 2).
5. PEI teachers' wages remain the second lowest in the country (BCTF 2012).
6. O. Dolbec, Executive Assistant, Quebec Provincial Association of Teachers (QPAT) in a telephone interview with the author, September 2012.
7. Nova Scotia, Québec, Manitoba and Alberta retain minimal local taxation.
8. Alberta Teachers' Association, Teacher Welfare Program department employee in a confidential telephone interview with the author, September 2012.
9. P. MacFadyen, Deputy General Secretary, Prince Edward Island Teachers' Federation in a telephone interview with the author, September 2012.
10. M. Caissie, labour relations officer, New Brunswick Teachers' Federation, in a telephone interview with the author, September 2012.
11. YTA (Yukon Teachers' Association) in a confidential email exchange with the author, September 2012.
12. A. Amirault, assistant executive director, Northwest Territories Teachers' Association, in a telephone interview with the author, October 2012.
13. T. Paci, Department Head, Manitoba Teachers Society Teacher Welfare, in a telephone interview with the author, September 2012.
14. R. Schmaltz, senior administrative staff member, Saskatchewan Teachers' Federation, in an email exchange with the author, September 2012.
15. In April 2011, the Supreme Court of British Columbia declared that the 2002 and 2004 legislation that stripped working conditions from teachers' collective agreements was unconstitutional (British Columbia Supreme Court 2011). L. Kuehn, Director of Research and Technology for the British Columbia Teachers' Federation shared this information in an email exchange with the author, September 2012.
16. The work-to-rule was a withdrawal of voluntary and extracurricular activities.
17. The provincial government announced the repeal of Bill 115 in January 2013 amid widespread protests by teachers' unions and their allies. However, the announcement was bittersweet for teachers' unions given that the bill had already been used to impose contracts and restrict the right to strike

9. THE PARADOX OF PROFESSIONALISM

Unions of Professionals in the Public Sector

Larry Savage and Michelle Webber

Unionized professional workers are one of the fastest growing segments of Canada's labour movement (Dobbie and Robinson 2008). These union members face unique political and workplace-based circumstances by virtue of their professional status, and as a result, their unions have traditionally adopted modes of organizing, bargaining and representation that are sometimes at odds with the mainstream labour movement's established *modus operandi*. Discourses of professionalism figure prominently in these unions, not only as tools to advance the professional interests of members but also as mechanisms in collective agreements designed to uphold standards in the workplace and in respective professions. Such a focus on professionalism gives these particular public sector unions a decidedly different flavour.

This chapter[1] is concerned with the ways in which discourses of professionalism serve to simultaneously mobilize and constrain union activism in the professional workplace. For unions of professional workers, such discourses can be effective at mobilizing resistance to workplace bureaucratization and deprofessionalization, but they also tend to constrain professional workers from engaging in militant or other forms of resistance that are understood as "unprofessional." We argue this paradox of professionalism has important implications for understanding the unique and complex political approaches and workplace strategies employed by professional unions in an era of neo-liberal restructuring and government austerity. Drawing on relevant primary sources and interviews with a wide variety of elected leaders, activists and staff representatives, we explore the nature of this paradox, its historical roots and its implications for the future in an effort to shed light on the understudied area of professional public sector unions in Canada.

In addition to analyzing relevant printed materials concerning the structure, practice and politics of professional unions in the public sector, this chapter draws on in-depth, qualitative, confidential interviews with

ten key informants. Our interviewees included current and former leaders, activists and staff at the Professional Institute of the Public Service
of Canada (PIPSC), the Association of Management, Administrative and
Professional Crown Employees of Ontario (AMAPCEO), the National Union
of the Canadian Association of University Teachers (NUCAUT), and the
International Federation of Professional and Technical Engineers (IFPTE).
The interviews focused primarily on professional union strategies and
approaches to certification, workplace representation and membership
mobilization. Interviewees were also asked about the relationship between
professionalism and unionization and links between professional unions and
the broader labour movement.

While each of the unions under consideration represents professional
workers in the Canadian public sector, they differ greatly in terms of size,
structure, membership and jurisdiction. With a membership of 57,000, PIPSC
is the second largest federal public service union in Canada and represents
scientists, engineers, architects, auditors, nurses and information technology professionals. AMAPCEO, the second largest union in the Ontario public
service, represents roughly 12,000 professional and supervisory employees.
NUCAUT represents unionized associations of postsecondary academic staff,
primarily university professors. As of 2012, twenty-one university faculty
associations across Canada were members of NUCAUT. IFPTE represents
roughly 8,000 professional and technical employees in Canada, including engineers, scientists, supervisors and finance specialists. Its chartered Canadian
locals include the Society of Energy Professionals, the Telecommunications
Employees Association of Manitoba and the Winnipeg Association of Public
Service Officers.

PROFESSIONALS AND UNIONS

While the term "professional" is certainly contested (Muzio, Kirkpatrick
and Kipling 2011; Evetts 2009a, 2009b), we borrow from sociological treat-
ments of professional workers by using heightened educational requirements,
specialized skills and an elevated perception of social class or prestige to
distinguish between professionals and other white-collar workers (Freidson
1994; Ritzer and Walczak 1986). We define professional unions as those
that represent a primarily professional workforce and work actively to brand
themselves as professional organizations.[2]

Professional unions come into existence for a variety of reasons and in
a number of ways. For some unions, like AMAPCEO, PIPSC and the Society
of Energy Professionals (Canada's largest IFPTE local), the process was quite
painless, with the state sanctioning and recognizing the union as a bargaining agent without much conflict or confrontation.[3] For others, like the Saint
Mary's Faculty Association, a NUCAUT affiliate, and the Saskatoon Civic

Middle Management Association (an independent union), certification was a strategy designed to insulate an existing professional association from being "raided" by a bona fide labour union. In the former case, the Canadian Union of Public Employees' campaign to organize university professors played a key role in convincing the Canadian Association of University Teachers to become involved in collective bargaining (Savage 1994: 57). Tellingly, according to Savage (ibid.), a survey of unionized Canadian professors in the 1970s revealed that the "great majority were opposed to collective bargaining in principle but thought the particular circumstances of their university justified it." In other cases, like the certification drives of the Telecommunications Employees Association of Manitoba in 1986 (TEAM 2012), or faculty associations at Brock or Queen's university in the mid 1990s (Rastin 2000; Savage, Webber and Butovsky 2012), professionals organized in response to workplace changes that required the strength and legal protections that only a certified labour union could provide.

Despite this variation, it is clear that most professional unions do not share the militant history of many industrial labour organizations that shed blood, sweat and tears to build their unions, win them recognition and defend their continued existence. This alternate history has certainly coloured the approach of professional unions in the realm of labour relations. Typically cast as strong adherents of business unionism, professional unions are often portrayed as preferring conciliation over confrontation at the bargaining table. Critics complain that professional unions tend to avoid labour disruptions at all costs, engage in very limited, if any, political action and do not generally identify with broader working-class struggles (confidential interviews). While there is unquestionably some truth to these characterizations, the reality of contemporary professional unions is far more complex.

PROFESSIONALISM, DEPROFESSIONALIZATION AND PROFESSIONAL WORK

Unionization and professionalism are often presented as incompatible in the academic literature (Crain 2004; Hurd 2000; Schlachter 1976). For example, Crain (2002: 598) argues that "the anti-individualist philosophy that characterizes traditional forms of unionism is obviously an uneasy fit with the ideology of professionalism" that stresses loyalty and a harmony of interest between professional workers and the organizations for which they work. In such a context, collective bargaining is viewed as needlessly confrontational and strikes are considered both unprofessional and unethical (Schlachter 1976: 458). Hurd (2000: 4) argues that some professional workers fear that standardized work rules, as prescribed by collective agreements, will unduly mechanize and restrict the work of professionals. Hurd (2000: 5) further argues that "provisions that protect members from arbitrary treatment may indirectly undermine professional standards by conferring job security on less

116

competent workers." Furthermore, Crain (2004: 544) argues that, historically, "professionals' monopoly power over knowledge furnished sufficient leverage that legislation or unions to protect against abuses of power by employers seemed superfluous," while Schlachter notes the argument that unions lacked the experience or expertise to represent the nonmonetary interests of professional workers, such as workplace "autonomy, occupational integrity and individual career satisfaction" (Schlachter 1976: 461).

Alexander (1980: 476), on the other hand, argues that aspects of unionization and professionalization are "complementary and reinforcing," arguing that both are "processes that represent collective, protective efforts on behalf of their membership and aimed at upward social mobility." For example, in a higher education context, Savage (1994: 58) argues that "collective bargaining made collegiality real. Faculty and administrators now met as legal equals at the bargaining table, no longer as beggars and supplicants." Some have gone even further, suggesting that unions of professionals effectively combat the trend toward deprofessionalization by helping to uphold professional autonomy, authority and work standards (Raelin 1989: 101).

While it is true that for a minority of professional workers professionalism was always considered compatible with unionization, most professionals viewed unions as leading to deprofessionalization (Raelin 1989:104). However, the early presumed juxtaposition of unionization and professionalism grossly underestimated organized labour's ability to represent the employment interests of a wide spectrum of professional workers in such a way that preserved their particular individualized character. For example, the standardized wages, work practices and seniority-based provisions that are central to traditional collective agreements are either secondary concerns or altogether absent in the collective agreements negotiated by the professional unions under examination here. In the university sector, for example, professors more or less negotiate starting salaries on an individual basis, and promotions rely primarily on a system of peer review, not seniority. Tellingly, the extremely high level of union density in Canadian universities suggests that unions have adapted very well to these long-standing individualized aspects of the academic workplace.

A key theme in the literature on professionals and unions is the sense that professional workers see themselves as sharing very little in common with other unionized workers. Gunderson (1979: 115) argues that solidarity in professional unions is often based on a sense of "occupational prestige" and "aloofness" that allows professionals to "distinguish themselves as something apart from other workers." Several interviewees picked up on this theme, describing their unions in opposition to their nonprofessional counterparts in the same sector. This dynamic was most apparent in the cases of AMAPCEO and PIPSC; both unions have members who have managerial authority over members of the Ontario Public Service Employees Union and the Public Service Alliance of Canada, respectively.

Crain (2004: 597) argues that professional workers' unwillingness to sacrifice class privilege and status is a key factor in explaining their historical reluctance to forge alliances with the broader labour movement. This traditional lack of solidarity reinforces the idea among union activists that professional unions are inward-looking, conservative, sectionalist and share more in common with employers than with other unionized workers (confidential interviews).

However, this characterization of professional unions is contested and will likely continue to be shaken as increased bureaucratization of the professional workplace, in pursuit of "efficiency" and "profitability," changes what it means to do professional work (Crain 2004: 597). As Crain (ibid.) argues, "when professional autonomy and expertise are subordinated to management control in the quest for profit maximization, professionals' very identity as professionals is jeopardized." Professionalism under these conditions "becomes primarily an ideological consolation used by employers to accommodate professional workers' needs for status privileges or a negotiating device used by professionals themselves to justify wages and privileges that differ from those of other workers" (Derber 1982: 16). Writing in the context of teacher unionism but certainly applicable to a much broader cross-section of professional workers in the public sector, Warburton (1986: 213) argues that discourses of professionalism represent "a dynamic element in their situation which both they and the state exploit as part of [a] dialectic of control and resistance." Such a dialectic is best understood as a paradox for professional unions. Not only do these unions shape and promote the professionalist discourses that help to advance the workplace-based professional interests of their members, but they also internalize many traits that primarily serve the interests of employers in the name of professionalism — respect for authority, loyalty to the institution and styles of dress (Rispel and Schneider 1991: 119).

When deployed by an employer, a discourse of professionalism, with a focus on customer service, performance targets and vertical accountability, becomes a central organizational objective in the workplace and acts as a "powerful mechanism for promoting occupational change and social control" (Evetts 2005: 3). Increased bureaucratization and standardization, often viewed by workers as threats to professional autonomy, are promoted and justified by senior management as ways of improving the level of professionalism (ibid.: 5).

However, discourses of professionalism are not confined to employers and unions. Evetts (2009a: 24) reminds us that professionalism, as a discourse of self-control, "can also be interpreted as an ideology which enables self-motivation and sometimes even self-exploitation." In her study of unionized professional engineers, Coulter (2009: 5) echoes the views of many of our interviewees when she argues that members "understood themselves to be 'professionals' and there was a widespread recognition of the need for voluntary overtime as part of their commitment." In addition, it is clear from our interviews that many professional workers view their work as primarily a social good or calling rather than an employment obligation. As one of our interviewees put it, professional workers' "level of understanding of themselves as union members or as members of the working class, broadly understood, is not very high" (confidential interview).

STRATEGIES AND INSTITUTIONAL CHARACTERISTICS OF PROFESSIONAL UNIONS

Tellingly, professional unions almost never refer to themselves as unions. Despite holding collective bargaining rights and all the other legal protections afforded by formal union certification, professional unions prefer the language of "association," "society" or "institute" to describe their organizations. The term "union," they argue, is alien to their members' workplace culture or social status, conjuring up images of unskilled industrial workers engaging in militant labour disruption. In many unionized professional workplaces, grievances become "disputes" and union stewards are replaced with "advocates" or dispute resolution "officers" who are cast as "reasonable" people who can sit down with management and work out problems in a calm, productive and nonadversarial manner (confidential interviews).

In a similar break with the more solidaristic culture of the mainstream labour movement, members of professional public sector unions eschew the singing of "Solidarity Forever" at conventions and do not use the terms "brother" and "sister" to refer to one another at meetings (confidential interviews). In part, the above reflects a rejection of a certain type of labour solidarity that considers workers' collective interests as standing in opposition to employer interests.

Strikes among professional unions are relatively rare, owing in part to a combination of low levels of militancy and radicalism among professional workers and member concerns over how a labour dispute might hurt the constituencies that depend on them (confidential interviews). Members of AMAPCEO and PIPSC have never been on strike. Conversely, strikes among faculty associations are becoming more common.[4]

In the realm of political mobilization, professional unions tend to rely on resource-heavy public education campaigns, designed to inform the public about the issues and underscore the importance of the jobs performed by members of professional unions. For example, in April 2012, a coalition of six professional public sector unions (PIPSC, the Association of Canadian Financial Officers, the Canadian Association of Professional Employees

[CAPE], the Association of Justice Counsel, the Canadian Federal Pilots Association and the Professional Association of Foreign Service Officers) launched the Professionals Serving Canadians campaign to highlight the negative aspects of proposed federal service job cuts (Professionals Serving Canadians 2012). These professional unions used the campaign to strategically project themselves as organizations that are equally concerned with the quality of public services and the conditions of public sector work.

While professional unions have stepped up these types of political awareness campaigns in recent years amid unprecedented neoliberal government restructuring, they have steered clear of engaging in partisan electoral politics. Miller (1971: 237) argued in the 1970s that professional employees, "if not legally prohibited from political action, may still feel that adverse political activities that pit them against a government party are inappropriate." Over the course of the last forty years, despite loosened restrictions on the political rights of public sector workers, this tradition of nonpartisan political action has largely remained intact. This strategic decision is no doubt rooted in tradition and the unique relationship between professional workers and the state but is also reinforced by the idea that "professionals" ought not to engage in the kinds of party-union relationships familiar to many blue-collar unions (confidential interviews). None of the unions examined in this chapter share any formal partisan links with political parties.

While professional unions have been adverse to participating in formal partisan politics, they have increasingly asserted a role for themselves in the public policy arena in an effort to influence the political environment in which collective bargaining unfolds. For example, university faculty associations routinely seek to influence public policy in the realm of higher education, while professional engineers in Ontario have taken public stands on energy issues (confidential interviews). Most of this activity occurs through lobbying or advertising (confidential interviews). Extraparliamentary activism, in the form of demonstrations or rallies, is not unheard of, but as the *Toronto Star*'s Tim Harper (2011) observed about members of the PIPSC:

> Even when they protest, they do it politely, and by the rules. Some 400 of them marched to Parliament Hill on Friday on their lunch hour, pounded their thunder sticks, then were sent back to their convention with a resounding cry to remain on the sidewalks so as not to impede traffic.

THE SHIFTING LANDSCAPE OF PROFESSIONAL UNIONS

Professional public sector workers are in some ways more insulated from the type of reverse class resentment arguments highlighted elsewhere this volume, largely because the elevated salary levels enjoyed by professional workers are generally not crafted as the product of unionization but rather as the result of meeting the stringent educational requirements typically associated with professional occupations (confidential interviews). In other words, professional workers are viewed as having "justifiably" earned their salaries and other entitlements. However, even this line of defence is proving difficult to buttress amid unprecedented austerity measures in the Canadian public sector.

In the past, some professional unions survived on "cultivating relationships with benevolent cabinet ministers" and therefore did not need to develop any sort of culture of membership mobilization or political action, secure in the knowledge that "mediation and arbitration rule the day and we would never strike" (confidential interview). Professionals often view arbitration as the best method of resolving disputes precisely because it appeals to their deference to expert knowledge and judgment. However, neoliberal restructuring has worked to undermine this long-standing perception by making it clear that "having the best arguments" is no substitute for concrete bargaining power in the face of an intransigent employer (confidential interview).

There is no question that grappling with public sector employers' shift toward more hard line concessionary bargaining has in many ways caught professional unions off guard. One interviewee described the typical approach to collective bargaining in the professional workplace as follows:

> We sit down with [management] and we joke about this and that and how our golf game is ... and they respect us and we respect them, and we're professionals and so we're not going to do anything hasty like strike or do anything to embarrass them and then they're going to give us our due and that's how it works. And that's how bargaining worked for a very, very long time, and they've been just so confused over the last few years, why they're not being treated that way anymore. (confidential interview)

Once shielded from some of the worst aspects of neoliberal public policy changes and cutbacks in the 1990s, union appeals to professional status are increasingly ignored by public sector employers, thus forcing professional unions to develop new tactics and strategies that bring them closer in line with the "mainstream" labour movement.

This contention is supported by the fact that three of the four professional unions examined in this chapter are now affiliated to the Canadian Labour Congress (CLC). In 1994, former Canadian Association of University Teachers (CAUT) president Roland Penner predicted that faculty unions would never affiliate to union centrals (Penner 1994: 50). However, just a few years later, he would be proven wrong. In 2001, NUCAUT was established for the specific purpose of creating an avenue for faculty unions to affiliate to the CLC. As of 2012, twenty-one faculty associations across Canada have joined

NUCAUT, including Penner's own University of Manitoba (NUCAUT 2012).

After having debated the issue in 1997 and 2010, PIPSC affiliated to the CLC at the national level in 2011 after a long process of consultation with members. The union made the decision to link up with the CLC after reaching the conclusion that it lacked the capacity to defend its own individual interests in the face of an "ideologically-driven agenda to shrink the public sector" and "a fiscal crisis that continues to deepen as a result of tax-cutting and the recession" (PIPSC 2011: 6). The move was made amid a realization that these unprecedented challenges demand "a new collective and cooperative approach with allies in public sector unions and the broader Canadian Labour movement" and a very sober acknowledgement that "the collegial relations and mutual respect we have cultivated [with the employer] in the past may not be the best strategy to protect and advance our members' interests in the current context" (ibid.).

While AMAPCEO and other professional unions like the Canadian Association of Professional Employees (CAPE)[5] remain unaffiliated with the CLC, being on the outside of the CLC has become the exception rather than the rule for professional unions.[6] In addition to PIPSC, NUCAUT and IFPTE, the Air Line Pilots Association and the Canadian Federation of Nurses Unions are CLC affiliates (PIPSC 2011: 7).

One of the reasons divisions between professional unions and other unions have narrowed considerably in recent decades has to do with the changing demographic composition of the labour movement itself. As the PIPSC discussion paper on affiliation to the CLC describes, Canada's "unionized work force has become increasingly educated and professional ... Public sector workers make up 56% of the CLC's membership and approximately 65% of CLC members have a post-secondary education" (PIPSC 2011: 7). In other words, the reality of the Canadian labour movement no longer reflects the popular cultural image of the male, hard-hatted, private-sector industrial worker — an image that professional workers were never comfortable embracing. However, while members of professional unions have seemingly grown comfortable with the specific union culture of their own organizations and have shown a willingness to join central labour organizations like the CLC as a way of defending their employment interests, whether professional unions will develop an advanced appreciation for more militant forms of collective action and labour solidarity remains an open question.

Unionized professional workers, especially those who have lived through a strike or lockout, unsurprisingly are most predisposed to embrace a more militant approach. For example, in the run-up to their historic 2005 strike against Hydro One, leaders of the Society of Energy Professionals sensed the labour relations terrain was shifting beneath their feet. The union's apolitical history and complete lack of rank-and-file activism left the Society incredibly vulnerable at the bargaining table. Politically, government-initiated privatization schemes helped to buttress concessionary demands by Ontario's energy sector. Given this context, the Society began reaching out for labour movement allies as part of a coordinated strategy to activate members in defence of their employment interests. The Society joined the IFPTE, and in turn the Canadian Labour Congress and Ontario Federation of Labour, in advance of the strike and hired organizers to mobilize members, who gradually developed their own leadership capacities. The successful strike, fought primarily over the issue of a proposed two-tiered salary structure for new hires, was viewed as being in response to an "unprovoked attack from management" (Coulter 2009: 8). According to Coulter (ibid.), "members felt [the proposed two-tier salary structure] was disrespectful to new hires, particularly young engineers being hired right out of university, an insult to them as professionals, and an insult to engineering as a profession." The 105-day strike unquestionably radicalized the workers, prompting them to engage in tactics that are outside the norm for professional unions. Society members interrupted the premier's speech at a meeting of the Association of Municipalities of Ontario, and some participated in a sit-in at the Toronto Board of Trade (ibid.:10). Overall, it was a

> remarkable case of worker militancy ... The engagement of so many workers for so long ... is noteworthy, but even more so because this was a group of workers that had little experience with political strike action, and no history of union consciousness. (ibid.: 11)

There are other examples of more confrontational tactics emerging amongst professional public sector unions. In July 2012, PIPSC members participated in a "Death of Evidence" demonstration on Parliament Hill in opposition to the federal government's muzzling of scientists (Pedwell 2012) and followed up several months later with unprecedented demonstrations and marches in Halifax, Toronto and Winnipeg in defence of federal public services. Similarly, in September 2012, thousands of AMAPCEO members gathered at Queen's Park for a rally in opposition to the premier's threat to impose a wage freeze and legislate a new contract. While AMAPCEO eventually reached a negotiated settlement that included a number of concessions, the union's unprecedented mobilization increased member militancy and raised expectations, as evidenced by the fact that 29 percent of members voted against ratification. In a media release, AMAPCEO president Gary Gannage acknowledged the union had taken a hit but signaled his intention to redouble AMAPCEO's efforts to organize and to build the capacity of members year round "to prepare to take any necessary action in the next round of bargaining" (AMAPCEO 2012). Gannage also acknowledged the need to work in common cause with "the labour movement and the community sector to

prevent the enactment of wrong-headed laws that jeopardize our constitutional rights and undermine the interests of all public sector workers" (ibid.).

These examples of recent militancy are not meant to suggest that these
unions have undergone some sort of radical transformation as a result of
recent strikes, demonstrations or mobilizations. Rather, they underscore how
wide the parameters of professionalist ideology can be stretched for union
purposes in defence of perceived professional entitlements, particularly as
these come under greater pressure.

THE FUTURE OF PROFESSIONAL UNIONS IN THE PUBLIC SECTOR

A combination of deteriorating working conditions, encroachments on
professional autonomy and a seemingly never-ending cycle of government
austerity will undoubtedly continue to draw unions and public sector professional workers closer together.

While professional unions are unquestionably diverse, what they share
in common is a professionalist orientation and discourse that informs their
general outlook on labour relations and unionism more broadly. Unions of
professionals have very effectively integrated "professional" issues (standards,
ethics, autonomous discretion, codes of conduct, provisions for individual
merit increases) into collective agreements in a way that complements professionalist notions and aspirations.

However, such a discursive frame of professionalism is used paradoxi-
cally by unions and employers to both motivate and constrain professional
workers. Specifically, the collective bargaining gains of professional workers
have come hand in hand with the general expectation that professional workers will not "abuse" such gains by engaging in "unprofessional" behaviour.

Crain (2004: 544) argues that "professionals who once shunned unions
as the antithesis of professionalism are now embracing them, seeking protection from the labor laws against the effects of commodification." However,
unions of professional workers who view labour relations as simply a legal,
rather than a political, process will ultimately discover that the neoliberal
assault on public sector professions threatens the very identity and autonomy
of professional workers, whether unionized or not.

In this context, mobilizing members around their professional occupational identities does have important limitations that must be acknowledged.
Such mobilization tactics could actually prove counterproductive in efforts to
forge broader working-class alliances between professional workers and their
nonprofessional counterparts by reinforcing the "separate" and "distinct"
character of professional unions. A strong focus on professional occupational
identity also risks giving professional workers a false sense of class position.
While Canada's working class is unquestionably highly stratified, none of
the members of professional unions considered in this chapter actually fit

the classic three-part definition of a professional (self-employed, self-directed, and bound by a code of ethics). Members of professional unions generally work for a fixed salary, answer to a boss and while they may have some flexibility in terms of the direction of their work, they are ultimately bound by collective agreements.

Nevertheless, it is clear that the unions studied in this chapter very much identify as professional organizations representing professional workers. This sectionalist impulse, however, need not necessarily foster a strict business union mentality for professional unions. This chapter has demonstrated that, despite their less adversarial character and more conservative political orientation, professional unions have come a long way over the course of the last two decades. While the professional identity of these workers clearly works to constrain sustained militancy, it can and has been used to organize and mobilize professionals in pursuit of professional standards of care and service for the publics they serve. The challenge for professional unions, then, is how to deploy discourses of professionalism to move beyond a strategy of self-preservation in the face of neoliberal restructuring with a view to elevating the public good as a whole, rather than the narrow occupational entitlements of individual professional workers.

Notes

1. This research was partly funded by the Social Sciences and Humanities Research Council of Canada (SSHRC).
2. For a discussion of other occupational groups sometimes included in the "professional" category, see Briskin's chapter on nurses and Hanson's chapter on teachers, both in this volume.
3. PIPSC was recognized as a certified union in 1967 following the implementation of the *Public Service Staff Relations Act*, and the Society of Energy Professionals and AMAPCEO were recognized as certified unions by Ontario's NDP government following voluntary recognition agreements in 1991 and 1995 respectively.
4. There were twelve faculty association strikes in the 1980s, ten in the 1990s and nineteen between 2000 and 2009 (NUCAUT 2012a, personal communication).
5. CAPE is the third largest federal public service union in Canada and represents analysts and research assistants at the Library of Parliament and translators, interpreters and social science services employees.
6. As of June 2013, AMAPCEO was actively considering affiliation to the CLC.

10. FEDERAL PUBLIC SECTOR UNIONS IN TIMES OF AUSTERITY
Linking Structure and Strategic Choice

Rosemary Warskett

For the fourth time in the last three decades, federal public sector workers and their unions are faced with austerity measures. This time the measures are significant and varied, coming in the form of layoffs; cuts to programs; privatization and contracting out; concession bargaining; denial of the right to strike; and pension changes that will weaken the defined benefit plan. With the re-election of the Harper Conservatives with a majority government in 2011, nobody is particularly surprised that the current government has turned to austerity and is cutting the federal public service by over 19,000 positions, gutting social and cultural programs and increasing public-private partnerships. More surprising, however, is the lack of a coordinated fightback by federal public sector unions. The Canadian Union of Postal Workers (CUPW), now 54,000 strong, has been dealing since 2011 with the aftermath of the removal of the right to strike and trying to avoid an imposed arbitrated contract. As for the Public Service Alliance of Canada (PSAC), the largest union in the federal public sector with approximately 180,000 members, it seems to have fallen into a period of quiescence, which stands in contrast to its militant actions during the 1980s and 1990s.

The federal public sector includes the Professional Institute of the Public Service of Canada (PIPSC) with 60,000 members, followed by a host of smaller unions including Canadian Association of Professional Employees (5,000 members), Canadian Air Traffic Controllers Association (2,000 members), Professional Association of Foreign Service Officers (1,600 members) together with a small number of workers in blue collar unions. CUPW and PSAC, however, are the main union players in the sector, setting the pattern that other unions have followed.

PSAC and CUPW are the main focus of this chapter,[1] not only because they represent the majority of nonprofessional members in the federal public sector but also because they have the most potential to mount a militant fightback against the current austerity measures. The main purpose of this chapter is to examine the strategic choices made by both PSAC and CUPW in fighting austerity measures. It is argued that the type of union and collective bargaining structure that was historically constructed is of crucial importance in both hindering and encouraging the formation of militant union action and has a direct impact on union strategy and the kind of solidarity that is constructed. Furthermore, the labour relations structure that the union operates within is a contributing factor in making strategic choices and, as a consequence, the construction of solidarity, union capacity and power. Union and labour law structures are not the only factors influencing the choices made, but they must be taken into account when assessing unions' potential to fight back against the current austerity measures.

STRATEGIC CHOICE AND UNION STRUCTURE

Ironically, at this moment of the most profound crisis of capital since the 1930s, the Canadian working class is in a state of disorganization. With low rates of unionization in the private sector, public sector unions remain a beacon of hope in the fightback against current attacks on unions and the working class in general. But most public sector unions seem on the defensive and unable to mobilize their members effectively. A solid fightback requires building solidarity across the union movement and with the working class broadly defined (Swartz and Warskett 2012: 20–21). What is needed is a union movement that has the power and capacity to mount an effective struggle against austerity measures, privatization and neoliberal discourse that claims the private sector will always be more efficient, better organized and more able to undertake the services that are publicly provided. Hurley and Gindin (2011) go further and argue that we need to rethink the very nature of the union movement. This means undertaking "this struggle in new ways and … re-evaluating everything about our own structures, processes and strategies … It essentially involves, to put it bluntly, a revolution inside our unions" (Hurley and Gindin 2011: 1–2).

If we are to rethink the very nature of the union movement, it is important to think about union structure in a dynamic historical relationship with strategic choices. The kind of structure unions put in place is itself a strategic choice resulting from earlier conflicts and struggles. This choice limits or expands the possibility of developing strategies that build the capacity of unions to develop solidarity within their ranks, across the labour movement and with other social movements. The dynamic relationship between strategies and structure can result in lesser or greater sectionalism and lesser or greater solidarity within and between unions.[2]

The founding moment of a union is of crucial importance to how union members construct future struggles. Union members make their own history,[3] but how they advance the union's collective goals and struggles must be in keeping with its constitutional rules and structure. Structures put in place at founding moments both limit and open up possibilities for union action and struggle, including making future changes to the structure itself. In examining union structure we need to ask: Does it encourage membership mobilization and democratic participation, or rather does it tend toward the union leadership and hired experts making decisions isolated from the membership? How does the structure relate to the process of collective bargaining and the potential to use strike power? How difficult is it to change the structure; is it open to change as new circumstances arise?

From its inception, PSAC's structure was top heavy with leaders distanced from the membership. When they formed PSAC in 1966 out of the merger of the Civil Service Association and the Civil Service Federation, its founders did not intend to form a labour union, let alone a militant union, but rather an "organic unity among all staff associations" (CSFC 1965: Resolution 353). The name itself — the Public Service Alliance of Canada — suggests a grouping of public sector staff associations rather than a union, and its founding structure was a victory for the federation.

The Civil Service Federation was a collection of staff associations that was a mirror image of the federal government departmental system. In contrast, the Civil Service Association was based on occupational groups that were found in every department. When the two differently structured staff associations merged, the various departmental associations became components of PSAC, creating a three-tiered structure. PSAC as the bargaining agent was the equivalent of Treasury Board, the employer, whereas the seventeen components mirrored their departmental management. The lower tier was made up of locals, but they were locals of the components not of PSAC.[4] This means that delegates elected at the local level go first to component convention and then may be elected to go to the PSAC convention, resulting in a final decision-making body far removed from the membership.

Structurally there was and remains an internal contradiction: the PSAC collectively bargains with Treasury Board for a large range of occupational groups that cross component lines, while the components' role is to consult with departmental managers, their role before the merger in 1966. This means that solidarity was and continues to be built around the component, not around the collective bargaining process and the capacity to strike. This often means that PSAC members have a strong identification with their department and the public services they provide,[5] but to this day PSAC struggles during the collective bargaining process to forge solidarity across component lines. There have been some changes to the structure of the federal government with the creation of government agencies and, as a consequence, to the PSAC structure, but for the most part sectionalism continues to occur within PSAC through division and conflict created by the component system.

From its beginning CUPW was very differently structured. In 1965, the Canadian Postal Employees Association (CPEA) transformed itself into a fighting union, in part as a result of the militant strike postal workers had undertaken earlier that year. The Federal Association of Letter Carriers "followed suit rapidly by transforming itself into the Letter Carriers Union of Canada (LCUC)" (Hoogers 2009: 1). In stark contrast to the other staff associations at that time, both CUPW and LCUC demonstrated they were prepared to take a militant stance. In fact, the postal unions' strike actions resulted in changes to the proposed *Public Service Staff Relations Act* (*PSSRA*) that earlier had only allowed for binding arbitration to settle collective bargaining disputes. After the 1965 postal workers' strike, the proposed legislation was rapidly changed to include the conciliation/strike route (Warskett 1997: 142–6).

The 1965 strike also made apparent the inadequacy of the CUPW union structure. It "had inherited a constitution and structure reflecting the milieu of the old Association where any improvements in wages or benefits required a cap-in-hand posture before government officials" (Hoogers 2009: 1). The structure did not aid in member mobilization, was top heavy and had no real regional structure. At the 1971 CUPW convention, an extensive set of constitutional and structural changes were presented to the membership. These included "clearly defined and democratic local, regional and national structures with specific responsibilities geared to promoting the mobilization and unity of the membership" (ibid.: 2). The basic structural elements put in place in 1971 remain today, although numerous additional changes over the years have strengthened this structure and the members' ability to achieve the objectives of the union.

Prior to the CUPW 1971 constitutional changes, the hard-fought issue of part-timers was resolved. A decision was made at the male-dominated 1968 convention — reversing an earlier convention decision — to organize these lower paid, predominantly female workers, and in 1969 nearly ninety percent of them voted to join CUPW. It was a progressive strategic choice to bring these workers into the union and use CUPW's bargaining power to raise their classification and wages rather than oppose part-time work. Jean-Claude Parrot, later president of CUPW, wrote that "[o]ur fight was not to divide one group of workers from another: rather it was to stop the use of cheap labour" (Parrot 2005: 21). This early strategy against wage and classification sectionalism remains a CUPW policy objective that has been pursued in subsequent years. It included bargaining higher wages for part-timers and coders, both female-dominated groups, as well as male-dominated mail handlers and more recently, rural and suburban mail carriers. The impact of these strategic choices radically reduced wage differentials within the union. According to Julie White (1993: 72), "the wage gap between the lowest and highest paid workers in the bargaining unit was 35 percent in 1965, but this had been reduced to just 2 percent twenty years later in 1985." The above demonstrates that, throughout its history, CUPW has successfully worked to reduce sectionalism within the union, and its structure reflects this objective. In contrast, PSAC is one big union within the federal government administration with a substantial wage gap between the highest and lowest paid member, in part because of the large number of occupational groups and classifications in different federal departments, agencies and crown corporations and under provincial and territorial jurisdiction. Its structure, however, has also encouraged these divisions.

Since the 1980s, both CUPW and PSAC have faced repeated attacks by Liberal and Conservative federal governments. PSAC for the most part is severely hampered by a more restrictive labour relations regime, whereas CUPW, by nature of its crown corporation status achieved in 1981, operates under the more liberal *Canada Labour Code*. In the following sections the structural limitations, both internal and external, in building the capacity and solidarity of both unions will be examined in relation to key strategic choices the unions made since their inception.

LOOKING BACK ON AUSTERITY IN THE FEDERAL PUBLIC SECTOR, 1975–2005

The significant crisis of capital in the 1970s was one of corporate profitability and reflected the political and union/workplace strength the working class had gained in the postwar period (Panitch and Gindin 2012: 133–7). The aftermath of the crisis led to austerity measures, mainly in the public sector (Evans this volume; Panitch and Swartz this volume). CUPW's reputation for militancy was cemented during this period. Up to 1981, the union bargained under the restrictions of the *PSSRA*, resulting in Treasury Board refusing to negotiate on technological change and working conditions, which they deemed to be management rights. During the 1970s, CUPW's strike actions over automation within the post office finally culminated in the 1978 strike and the jailing of Jean-Claude Parrot. He was criminally charged with not telling postal workers to return to work "forthwith" once their strike was declared illegal (Parrot 2005: 118). Instead of damping militancy, the injustice of the CUPW president's criminal conviction brought support from some unions and seemed to have a radicalizing effect on PSAC members as well. However, while postal workers remained unbowed in the face of this coercion, when legislated back to work in subsequent years they obeyed the law for the most part. Both the shock of seeing their leader jailed and the threats of large fines for individual union members have had a profoundly disciplining effect on the CUPW membership and the union movement in general. Reflecting on being legislated back to work again in 1987, Parrot (ibid.: 204) notes: "We surprised a lot of people when we decided to go back to work after the passage of Bill C-86 but, as I said before, I've never been a willing candidate for suicide."

In the wake of the 1970s profitability crisis, the beginning of the 1980s produced high levels of inflation resulting in interest rates rising to over 20 percent in Canada, leading to Trudeau's Liberal government imposing legislative wage and price controls. While unions in the private sector continued to negotiate for the most part as usual, unions in the federal public sector experienced a two-year termination of collective bargaining (Swimmer 1995: 388). Just prior to these austerity measures, PSAC clerical workers (CRs), approximately 75 percent women, had circumvented the old male-dominated civil service leadership and undertaken unauthorized strike action. Organizing the CR strike meant mobilizing across component lines and building an ad hoc structure of strike captains and regional picket captains corresponding to work locations rather than component membership. It became glaringly apparent that the component structure was useless during a large strike and that the role of component leaders was consulting with departmental managers rather than mobilizing the membership. One of the consequences of the CR strike was that, by the mid 1980s, new activists, many of whom were women who had cut their teeth on the picket lines, were challenging the traditional leadership (Warskett 1997: 250–7).

The CR strike caused divisions within PSAC in part because of the development of a parallel structure of membership mobilization. This alternate structure of militancy was the main source of the component criticism (Warskett 1997: 226–35).[6] Once the strike ended, the temporary structure disappeared and the locals were once again under control of the components. But many of the strike activists challenged for leadership positions at all levels of the union and started to demand changes to the collective bargaining structure.[7]

In 1981, CUPW negotiated the end to a 42-day strike, a key victory of which was paid maternity leave. Seeing CUPW's gains, many PSAC activists started to push PSAC on a more militant path by advocating for all bargaining units to choose the conciliation/strike route rather than binding arbitration. The experience of the CR strike had revealed that to build greater solidarity and power there needed to be coordinated bargaining across all the Treasury Board bargaining groups. In 1985, delegates to the PSAC convention voted to mandate that occupational groups who participated in the master agreement were to be on the conciliation/strike route. This decision was strongly opposed by some component leaders but strongly supported by Daryl Bean, then president of PSAC. The culmination of this strategy was seven bargaining tables negotiating at the same time all with the possibility of using the strike weapon, instead of over thirty different occupational groups all with different bargaining timetables.

The election of the Mulroney Conservative government in 1984 ushered in a neoliberal trade agreement as well as austerity measures within the federal government, with Mulroney making the infamous threat that federal public employees would be given "pink slips and running shoes" (quoted in Zussman 1986: 255). But the Conservatives did agree to coordinated bargaining of all the groups, even if their "major concern was to introduce this process without increasing the unions' bargaining power" (Swimmer 1995: 391).

Unlike CUPW, which now bargained under the provisions of the *Canada Labour Code*, PSAC negotiated under the limitations imposed by the *Public Service Staff Relations Act* (later the *Public Service Labour Relations Act*) and the *Public Service Employment Act*. These two pieces of legislation together severely restrict bargaining issues; in particular, classification of positions and seniority are deemed non-negotiable. In addition, certain positions were designated as ineligible to strike because of the "safety and security of the public." Swimmer (1995: 381) points out that, after the strikes in the early 1980s, "60 percent of bargaining units (29 of 48) had more than half their members designated, and 35 percent had virtually everyone designated. The Liberal government apparently succeeded in removing the right to strike by the back door."

By 1991, the Conservatives increased neoliberal austerity measures and announced wage controls in the February budget. However, "by 1991, the PSAC had succeeded in obtaining a bargaining structure which would allow its 110,000 non-designated members to strike simultaneously" (Swimmer 1995: 392). That PSAC continued to mobilize its members toward a strike of all its seven bargaining groups despite austerity speaks to how far the union had come. The strike began in September 1991, and Parrot (2005: 220) recalls "that Ottawa was like a war zone ... picket lines were everywhere." This was remarkable given the high number of workers designated as nonstrikers. Clearly the designation process did not sufficiently damage the effectiveness of the strike given that eventually the union was legislated back to work. When the strike ended in October 1991, with large demonstrations in Ottawa and across the country, PSAC members went back to work with their heads held high.

The defeat of the Conservative government in 1993 ushered in the Chrétien/Martin Liberals. "In their first budget, the Liberals extended the wage controls, due to expire in 1995, for an additional two years" (Whitaker 2004: 75). This meant six consecutive years without the right to bargain. Deficit reduction took priority through "drastic staff reductions ... forcing departments to demonstrate why they, rather than the private, or voluntary sectors or the provinces, should be doing what they were doing" (ibid.). Under this initiative, approximately 56,000 federal positions were eliminated, resulting in a decline of 17 percent of the PSAC membership. Then as now, permanent employees (indeterminate) were protected by the Workforce Adjustment Program won by PSAC in the mid 1980s. This job security measure includes "six months' layoff notice, one year of salary protection for those forced to accept a lower paying job, and up to one year of retraining" (Swimmer 1995: 393). Seniority, however, plays no role in determining who is laid off, and workers often find themselves competing with other union members for a job. This process can be very damaging to solidarity during periods of cutbacks; the members affected by the workforce adjustment process are very reluctant to take militant action given their hope of finding another job in the federal government.

During the 1980s and 1990s, CUPW continued toward building one big union within Canada Post and also developed greater solidarity with community groups. They entered merger negotiations with the LCUC. After these fell through, a vote supervised by the Canada Labour Relations Board was held in early 1989. CUPW won the vote and doubled in size overnight (Hoogers 2009: 7). The merger also brought in members from the Union of Postal and Communications Employees (UPCE), a component of PSAC. Thus, when the postal workers went on strike in August 1991, it was with a large, strong bargaining unit. They had also extended their solidarity outside the union by signing solidarity pacts with community groups, committing to deliver cheques in the event of a strike[8] (Hurley and Gindin 2012: 3; Parrot 2005: 216–7). Once again, CUPW was legislated back to work but was able to make gains in a number of areas despite the imposed arbitration.

Within PSAC, membership pressure to change the union's structure resulted in the creation of regional structures that, it was argued, would bring the union much closer to the membership and reduce the power of the components. The 1997 PSAC triennial convention established both regional committees and a regional convention. While this change to the structure has resulted in increased membership activity through equity and political action committees, the main actors in these committees were still for the most part appointed by the components rather than being elected democratically by local members. As a consequence, the conservatizing pull of the component system remained in place for the most part.

During the late 1990s and into the 2000s, however, PSAC responded to the threats of privatization by organizing outside of its traditional membership. This has resulted in the growth of smaller regional bargaining units and of the number of members in directly chartered locals. While these smaller units have less bargaining power than the large Treasury Board units, they also experience a more "hands on" collective bargaining experience and greater control over negotiations.

In the 1990s, CUPW decided to work with the rural and suburban route mail carriers who were Canada Post independent contractors without the legal right to organize and bargain, a majority of them women. After a long, protracted organizing drive, by 2002 a majority of the carriers had signed up as CUPW members (Bourque and Bickerton 2004). In the 2004 round of bargaining, using the strength of its larger bargaining unit, CUPW "demanded that Canada Post make the couriers employees and no longer subject to the law excluding them from collective bargaining" (Clark and Warskett 2010: 248). The employer agreed to contract in the workers, making them employees of Canada Post. To get this agreement, however, CUPW gave up severance pay, resulting in dissent within the union. When the collective agreement was voted on in July 2003, only 68 percent voted for ratification, a much lower percentage than normal (Bourque and Bickerton 2004). Nevertheless, the solidarity shown toward the unorganized rural and suburban workers by the majority of CUPW members is a remarkable example of the kind of actions needed to build a new labour movement (Hurley and Gindin 2011: 3).

AUSTERITY UNDER THE HARPER CONSERVATIVES

Under the Harper Conservatives, it is clear that if any union in the federal public service has significant strike power it will be legislated back to work. For all intents and purposes, there is no right to strike if strike action causes the smallest public disruption. CUPW's 2010 dispute with Canada Post was quickly ended by legislation that imposed a wage increase that was less than Canada Post's last offer. This kind of coercion and discipline, together with the proposed layoffs, privatization and continual anti-union rhetoric, has sent a chill amongst PSAC and CUPW members.

It was in the midst of thousands of members receiving notice that their positions may be terminated that the PSAC's national triennial convention was convened in Ottawa at the end of April 2012. It quickly became apparent that the PSAC structure continued to act as a drag on the possibility of a militant fightback. This was made evident during the course of a debate on the third day of the convention concerning a resolution that, if passed, would have required all directly chartered locals to be assigned to a component (PSAC 2012b: 18). Not only has there been a decentralization of the federal government structure with the creation of separate government agencies such as Parks Canada, Border Services, taxation and the museums,[9] as well PSAC has organized outside its traditional federal government membership. In the last six years, approximately 30,000 nonfederal government workers have joined the union. A large contingent of these new members (20,000) is from Québec, mainly university teaching and research assistants. The presence of these new members was very apparent on the 2012 convention floor: they were wearing red squares in support of the Québec students' strike and made impassioned speeches at the microphones asking for support.

Many component leaders, however, expressed concern that these new members were organized into directly chartered locals and not into the component structure, seemingly fearful that a change in PSAC's structure would result. As one component president stated on the floor, "I don't like the way the structure is going." However, the resolution was lost by over 50 percent, far short of the two-thirds of the delegates required for a constitutional change. This defeat suggests that the component system is weakening, although it is likely to remain a source of internal division and infighting for some time to come. It is interesting to note that the convention also passed a resolution "to commence an organizing drive to reclaim all lost bargaining unit work" (PSAC 2012c: 11). This implies that PSAC will organize workers in jobs that have been privatized and contracted out. The addition of members outside the federal government will increase those in directly chartered locals and further contribute to lessening of component power. As well it will result in more members bargaining under legislation that is more liberal than the *PSSRA*.

Even though PSAC was under severe attack by the federal Conservatives, at the 2012 convention the fight over structure took precedence over fighting back against austerity.[10] The delegates seemed too absorbed by structural and financial matters to focus on any concrete strategy against austerity measures. No emergency resolution concerning a fightback strategy came to the floor, despite the daily reports from delegates about positions and programs being lost. There was no hint of the need for militant action, whether in the form of strikes or demonstrations. Debate over finances dominated the government austerity discussion; the focus was on launching a public relations campaign highlighting the need for public services over the next three years, resulting in a loud silence about mobilization and militant action by the membership against the cutbacks.

The lack of militancy was also apparent in the discussion about loss of membership and the possible loss of union dues. Eventually a resolution was passed in favour of an emergency levy if the membership drops below 170,000 in the next three years (it is currently over 180,000) and a substantial dues increase if membership drops below 140,000 (PSAC 2012a: B17). It appeared that PSAC had already accepted the loss of membership, but they were ensuring that the union — rather than the struggle — would continue. It is as if the convention was acknowledging the impossibility of mobilizing the membership against the cutbacks.

Despite CUPW's less debilitating structure, the gutting of its strike power seems to have caused divisions within the union. After CUPW's Urban Operations members returned to work in 2011, the leadership spent the following year and a half attempting to avoid final offer selection arbitration, in which the arbitrator must select either the union or employer proposal in its entirety. The union successfully challenged the appointment of two arbitrators, arguing that they were biased. In October 2012, they reached a tentative agreement that, while avoiding the worst of the employer's demands, nevertheless included concessions. The leadership's message to the membership was that "this settlement would be better than what we could get through final offer selection" (CUPW 2012). On January 31, 2013, it was reported that 57 percent of the Urban Postal Operations unit voted in favour of the agreement (CUPW 2013), an even lower acceptance rate than the prior disputed agreement.[11] Among CUPW activists there is widespread criticism of the settlement as well as the leadership's lack of attempt to mobilize the members and engage with labour and community groups against austerity measures.

CONCLUSION

When CUPW changed its name and became a union in 1965, there was recognition that it was no longer a staff association engaged in top-level consultations with the employer but rather a democratic union that was prepared to strike in support of collective bargaining demands if necessary. This strategic choice was reflected in constitutional changes made at the 1971 convention that resulted in a union structure designed to encourage mobilization, education and solidarity-building within the membership. It was also clear that CUPW intended to expand the union within Canada Post and work to keep wage differentials at a minimum. Looking back on its history, CUPW's objective of creating one big union in postal communications has clearly largely been achieved. Plus it was successful in acting in solidarity with several community groups. Nevertheless, at this point CUPW appears to have been somewhat beaten down by the attacks it has experienced over the last thirty years, especially on its right to strike. Compared to PSAC, however, it remains a more democratically structured union, and although CUPW's leadership seems to have retreated from mobilizing its membership and engaging community groups, nevertheless CUPW's structure leaves open the possibility of engaging in strategic discussions, at all levels of the union, about how to build alliances to fight future austerity measures.[12]

In contrast, at its inception in 1967, PSAC made a strategic choice to cement in place a component structure that ran counter to the collective bargaining process and counter to mobilizing the membership around collective bargaining and strike action. The contradictions inherent in its structure have acted as a drag on militancy and generated constant divisions within the union. The internal conflict generated by the component system continues to dominate PSAC conventions. But there are signs that the components' sectionalism is weakening. The victory by the directly chartered locals in defeating the motion requiring them to belong to a component means that there will likely be continued growth in locals outside the component system. This means that PSAC is developing into a different kind of union, one in which there is a greater number of bargaining units where the federal Treasury Board is no longer the employer and where the workers are not even within the federal public sector. Creating solidarity between these diverse kinds of workers presents a new challenge. Until PSAC makes a strategic choice to build solidarity across the units with the intention of mobilizing them against the neoliberal agenda and changing its constitution and structure to reflect this choice, internal battles and divisions will continue weakening its effectiveness as a union.

Perhaps for both PSAC and CUPW the recent attacks on federal public sector workers and public services will help to underline that no one union alone can successfully fight back against the neoliberal agenda. And that the development of a militant labour movement that builds alliances across unions and other social movements has never been more necessary.

Notes

1. I would like to thank Bob Allen, David Camfield, Dale Clark, Evert Hoogers, Stephanie Ross, Larry Savage and Donald Swartz for their very helpful comments on an earlier draft.

2. The way in which sectionalism impedes the development of solidarity is discussed by Swartz and Warskett (2012: 21) where they point out that "sectionalism is the tendency to limit the culture of solidarity to a specific group of workers."

3. This section draws upon Karl Marx's historical analysis in *The Eighteenth Brumaire of Louis Bonaparte* where he famously noted that "Men make their own history, but they do not make it just as they please; they do not make it under circumstances chosen by themselves, but under circumstances directly encountered, given and transmitted from the past" (Marx 1970: 96).

4. One way of thinking of this confusing union structure is that most occupational groups certified as bargaining units cut across component lines, whereas a few occupational groups were found only in one component. For example, clerical workers (CRs) were members of all seventeen components, whereas prison guards were found only in one component.

5. For example, members of the Canadian Employees and Insurance Union acted in solidarity with the unemployed during the early 1990s by producing pamphlets that informed people how to apply for unemployment insurance and not be disqualified (McElligott 2001; Hurley and Gindin 2011: 4). Bill Doherty, vice-president of PSAC during the 1970s and '80s, wrote: "If the Alliance had been human, it would have been committed long ago because of a severe and crippling form of schizophrenia" (Doherty 1978: 1).

6. Certain components took a more militant stance than others, such as the Canadian Employment and Insurance Union.

7. Nycole Turmel, who later became the first woman president of PSAC, first became active in the union during the CR strike.
8. Examples of these groups were the National Anti-Poverty Organization, Disabled People for Employment Equity, Canada Council of Retirees, Ontario Coalition against Poverty and the Canadian Federation of Students.
9. Members in these agencies remain part of the component system but are certified and bargain as separate PSAC bargaining groups.
10. I was an observer at the convention and what follows is from my notes.
11. At the same time it was reported that the Rural and Suburban Mail Couriers (RSMC) has accepted their tentative agreement by 67 percent. This group did not go on strike, and although the acceptance rate is higher than those voting for the Urban Postal Operations, the lower than normal acceptance rate points to some dissatisfaction with the current leadership.
12. Email correspondence with Dale Clark, past president of CUPW.

REFERENCES

Alberta Court of Appeal. 1984. *Re Public Service Employees Act, Labour Relations Act and Police Officers Collective Bargaining Act*, 16 D.L.R. (4th) 359.

Albo, G. and D. Crow. 2005. "Neo-liberalism, NAFTA, and the State of the North American Labour Movements." *Just Labour: A Canadian Journal of Work and Society* 6/7 (Autumn).

Albo, G., S. Gindin and L. Panitch. 2010. *In and Out of Crisis: The Global Financial Meltdown and Left Alternatives*. Oakland: PM Press.

Alexander, L. 1980. "Professionalization and Unionization: Compatible After All?" *Social Work* 25, 6 (November).

AMAPCEO (Association of Management, Administrative, Professional and Crown Employees of Ontario). 2012. "New Collective Agreement Ratified." News release, October 18. <amapceo.on.ca/mediareleases/news/RatifiedCollectiveAgreement.php>.

Annis, R. 2012. "B.C. Teachers Reach Two-Year Agreement with Government, Key Issues Unresolved." <rogerannis.com/bc-teachers-reach-two-year-agreement-with-government-key-issues-unresolved>. June 29.

Aptheker, B. 1989. *Tapestries of Life: Women's Work, Women's Consciousness, and the Meaning of Daily Experience*. Amherst: University of Massachusetts Press.

Archer, K. 1990. *Political Choices and Electoral Consequences: A Study of Organized Labour and the New Democratic Party*. Montreal: McGill-Queen's University Press.

Archer, K., and A. Whitehorn. 1997. *Political Activists: The NDP in Convention*. Toronto: Oxford University Press.

Armstrong, P. 2012. "Canadian Health Care: Privatization and Gendered Labour." *The Bullet* 595. <socialistproject.ca/bullet/595>. February 6.

Armstrong, P., and H. Armstrong. 2010. *Wasting Away: The Undermining of Canadian Health Care*. 2nd ed. Toronto: Oxford University Press.

Ashby, S. 2012. "Standing Up to the Corporate School Agenda, Chicago Teachers Greenlight Strike." *Labor Notes*. <labornotes.org/2012/06/standing-corporate-school-agenda-chicago-teachers-greenlight-strike>. June 12.

ATA (Alberta Teachers' Association). 2012. "How do Tripartite Talks Affect Bargaining?" <teachers.ab.ca/Publications/ATA%20News/Volume%2047%20 2012-13/Number-4/Pages/Creating-the-Conditions.aspx>. October 9.

Baines, D. 2010a. "Neoliberal Restructuring, Activism/Participation, and Social Unionism in the Nonprofit Social Services." *Nonprofit and Voluntary Sector Quarterly* 39, 1.

___. 2010b. "'In a Different Way': Social Unionism in the Nonprofit Social Services: An Australian-Canadian Comparison." *Journal of Labor Studies* 35, 4.

___. 2006. "'Staying with People Who Slap Us Around': Gender, Juggling and Violence in Paid and Unpaid Care Work." *Gender, Work and Organization* 13, 3.

___. 2004. "Seven Kinds of Work — Only One Paid: Raced, Gendered and Restructured Care Work in the Social Services Sector." *Atlantis: A Women's Studies Journal* 28.

Ballantyne, M., and S. Staples. 2012. "Labour Movement Must Be Defender of All Workers." *The Guelph Mercury*. <guelphmercury.com/opinion/columns/

article/790187--labour-movement-must-be-defender-of-all-workers>.
September 1.

Bank of Canada. n.d. "Consumer Price Index, 2000 to Present.".

Barnetson, B. 2010. "Alberta's 2002 Teacher Strike: The Political Economy of Labor
Relations in Education." *Education Policy Analysis Archives* 18, 3. <epaa.asu.edu/
epaa/v18n3/>.

BCFL (British Columbia Federation of Labour). 2012. "New Poll Shows B.C. Supports
Public Sector Workers." *B.C. Federationist.* <bcfederationist.com/watch-poll-
shows-bc-supports-public-sector-workers/>.

BCGEU (British Columbia Government and Service Employees' Union). n.d. "Quick
Facts about the BCGEU." <bcgeu.ca/news_centre_quick>.

B.C. Health Services. 2007. *Health Services and Support — Facilities Subsector Bargaining Assn.
v. British Columbia* [2007] 2 S.C.R. 391, SCC 27.

BCTF (British Columbia Teachers' Federation). n.d. "History of the BCTF." <bctf.
ca/uploadedFiles/About_Us/HistorySummary.pdf >.

___. 2012. "Canadian Teacher Salary Rankings: Provinces and Territories." <bctf.
ca/uploadedFiles/Public/BargainingContracts/2011-12SalaryRankings.pdf>.

Beitel, K. 2010. "The Crisis, the Deficit and the Power of the Dollar: Resisting the
Public Sector's Devaluation." In *Socialist Register 2011: The Crisis This Time*, ed.
L. Panitch, G. Albo and V. Chibber, 260–82. London: Merlin.

Benford, R.D., and D.A. Snow. 2000. "Framing Processes and Social Movements."
Annual Review of Sociology 26.

Benzie, R. 2009a. "McGuinty Accused of Betraying the Poor." *Toronto Star*, March 31.

___. 2009b. "As Government Deficit Soars, Restraint Looms." *Toronto Star*, October
22.

Bezanson, K., and M. Luxton (eds.). 2006. *Social Reproduction: Feminist Political Economy
Challenges Neo-Liberalism.* Toronto: University of Toronto Press.

Black, S. 2005. "Community Unionism: Strategy for Organizing in the New
Economy." *New Labor Forum* 14, 3.

Bleakney, D. 2011. "The Confines of Compromise." <briarpatchmagazine.com/
articles/view/the-confines-of-compromise>. November 1.

Bleyer, P. 1992. "Coalitions of Social Movements as Agencies for Social Change:
The Action Canada Network." *Organizing Dissent: Contemporary Social Movements
in Theory and Practice*, ed. W. Carroll, 102–17. Toronto: Garamond.

Bourque, D., and G. Bickerton. 2004. "Stepping Out of the Legal Framework:
Organizing Rural Route Couriers." Paper prepared for the International
Colloquium on Union Renewal, University of Montreal. November.

Braedley, S. 2009. "A Ladder Up: Ontario Firefighters' Wages in Neoliberal Times."
Just Labour 14 (Autumn).

___. 2006. "Someone to Watch over You: Gender, Class and Social Reproduction."
In *Social Reproduction: Feminist Political Economy Challenges Neo-Liberalism*, ed. K.
Bezanson and M. Luxton, 215–30. Toronto: University of Toronto Press.

Briskin, L. 2013. "Nurse Militancy and Strike Action." *Workers of the World: International
Journal on Strikes and Social Conflict* 1, 2.

___. 2012. "Resistance, Mobilisation and Militancy: Nurses on Strike." *Nursing
Inquiry* 19, 4.

___. 2011a. "Sites of Struggle/Vehicles of Resistance: Unions and Women Workers." In *Gendered Intersections: An Introduction to Women and Gender Studies*, ed. C.L. Biggs, P. Downe and S. Gingell. Halifax: Fernwood.

___. 2011b. "Union Renewal, Postheroic Leadership, and Women's Organizing: Crossing Discourses, Reframing Debates." *Labor Studies Journal* 36, 4.

___. 2011c. "The Militancy of Nurses and Union Renewal." *Transfer: European Review of Labour and Research* 17, 4.

___. 2007a. "CUPE on Strike, 1963–2004." *Just Labour: A Canadian Journal of Work and Society* 10 (Spring).

___. 2007b. "Public Sector Militancy, Feminization, and Employer Aggression: Trends in Strikes, Lockouts, and Wildcats in Canada from 1960 to 2004." In *Strikes around the World*, ed. H. Dribbusch, D. Lyddon, K. Vandaele and S. van der Velden. Amsterdam: Aksant.

___. 2006. "Victimization and Agency: The Social Construction of Union Women's Leadership." *Industrial Relations Journal* 37, 4.

Briskin, L., and P. McDermott (eds.). 1993. *Women Challenging Unions*. Toronto: University of Toronto Press.

British Columbia Supreme Court. 2011. *British Columbia Teachers' Federation v. British Columbia*. BCSC 469.

Britton, C. 2006. "A Historical Listing of Significant Events in Manitoba's Elementary-Secondary Education, Post-Secondary Education and Training Systems 1989–2006." University of Manitoba Faculty of Medicine. <umani-toba.ca/faculties/medicine/units/mchp/protocol/media/history_educa-tion_events_1989to2006.pdf>.

Brogan, P. 2012. "7 Days That Shook Chicago: The 2012 Chicago Teachers Strike." *The Bullet* 697. <socialistproject.ca/bullet/697.php>. September 21.

Bronskill, J. 2011. "Back-to-Work Bill in Postal Dispute Becomes Law." *The Canadian Press*, June 26.

Brown, G.D., A.M. Greaney, M.E. Kelly-Fitzgibbon and J. McCarthy. 2006. "The 1999 Irish Nurses' Strike: Nursing Versions of the Strike and Self-Identity in a General Hospital." *Journal of Advanced Nursing* 56, 2.

Byers, B. 2002. "Applying the Lessons to the Canadian Experience: Barb Byers, President, Saskatchewan Federation of Labour." In *Labour & Social Democracy: International Perspectives*, ed. P. Leduc Browne, 75–79. Ottawa: Canadian Centre for Policy Alternatives.

Camfield, D. 2012. "Les Services Publics Canadiens Pris d'Assaut." *Presse-Toi à Gauche*. <pressegauche.org/spip.php?article10650>. June 12.

___. 2011a. *Canadian Labour in Crisis: Reinventing the Workers' Movement*. Halifax: Fernwood.

___. 2011b. "Lessons of the Canada Post Lockout." *Fast Facts*. <policyalternatives. ca/publications/commentary/fast-facts-lessons-canada-post-lockout>. June 30.

___. 2011c. "The 'Great Recession,' the Employers' Offensive and Canadian Public Sector Unions." *Socialist Studies/Etudes Socialistes* 7, 1/2.

___. 2009. "Sympathy for the Teacher: Labour Law and Transgressive Workers' Collective Action in British Columbia, 2005." *Capital & Class* 33, 3.

___. 2007. "Renewal in Canadian Public Sector Unions: Neoliberalism and Union Praxis." *Relations Industrielles/Industrial Relations* 62, 2.

___. 2006. "Neoliberalism and Working-Class Resistance in British Columbia: The Hospital Employees' Union Struggle 2002–2004." *Labour/Le Travail* 57 (Spring).

___. 2005. "Renewing the Study of Public Sector Unions in Canada." *Socialist Studies* 1, 2.

Carniol, B. 2010. *Case Critical: The Dilemma of Social Work in Canada*. Toronto: Between the Lines.

Carroll, W.K., and R.S. Ratner. 2005. "The NDP Regime in British Columbia, 1991–2001: A Post-Mortem." In *Challenges and Perils: Social Democracy in Neoliberal Times*, ed. W.K. Carroll and R.S. Ratner, 105–36. Halifax: Fernwood.

Cassidy, M. 1986. "Political Rights for Public Servants: A Federal Perspective." *Canadian Public Administration* 29.

CBC News online. 2013. "McGuinty Seeks to Prevent 'Illegal' Teachers Strike Action." <cbc.ca/news/canada/windsor/story/2013/01/09/ontario-elementary-teachers-announce-political-protest.html?autoplay=true>. January 9.

___. 2012. "Gender Equality Case Nets Nurses $150m." <cbc.ca/news/canada/ottawa/story/2012/07/03/ottawa-nurses-in-public-service-win-150-million-dollar-settlement.html>. July 3.

___. 2011a. "Restrictions on B.C. Teachers Ruled Unconstitutional." <cbc.ca/news/canada/british-columbia/story/2011/04/13/bc-class-size-ruling.html>. April 13.

___. 2011b. "Planned School Board Cuts Anger Quebec Teachers." <cbc.ca/news/canada/montreal/story/2011/10/21/quebec-school-board-cuts.html>. October 21.

___. 2011c. "Teachers Begin 2-Day Strike in Sask." <cbc.ca/news/canada/saskatchewan/story/2011/05/25/sk-teacher-strike-1105.html>. May 25.

___. 2011d. "B.C. Teachers Give Strike Notice." <cbc.ca/news/canada/british-columbia/story/2011/08/31/bc-teachers-strike-student-impact.html>. August 31.

___. 1999. "Police Association Wants Liberal Ad Withdrawn." <cbc.ca/news/story/1999/05/26/onele_libas0525.html>. May 26.

CFLR (Canadian Foundation for Labour Rights). 2012. "Restrictive Labour Laws Directory." <labourrights.ca/restrictive-labour-laws>.

CFNU (Canadian Federation of Nurses Unions). 2012. "The Nursing Workforce: Canadian Federation of Nurses Unions Backgrounder." <nursesunions.ca/sites/default/files/2012.backgrounder.nursing_workforce.e_0.pdf>. February.

___. 2011. "Quick Facts: Trends in Own Illness or Disability-Related Absenteeism and Overtime among Publicly-Employed Registered Nurses." <nursesunions.ca/sites/default/files/overtime_and_absenteeism_quick_facts.pdf>. June.

___. n.d. "Member Organizations." <nursesunions.ca/member-organizations>.

CFNU/Nanos Research. 2009. "Canadians Want Government to Address Nursing Shortage, Health Care, in These Tough Economic Times, New Poll Finds." News release, June 8. <reuters.com/article/2009/06/08/idUS68607+08-Jun-2009+MW20090608>.

Charlesworth, S. 2010. "The Regulation of Paid Workers Wages and Conditions in the Nonprofit Sector: A Toronto Case Study." *Relations industrielles/Industrial Relations* 65, 3.

Clark, D., and R. Warskett. 2010. "Labour Fragmentation and New Forms of

Organizing and Bargaining in the Service Sector." In *Interrogating the New Economy: Restructuring Work in the 21st Century*, ed. N.J. Pupo and M.P. Thomas, 235–55. Toronto: University of Toronto Press.

Clarke, J. 2004. "Dissolving the Public Realm? The Logics and Limits of Neo-Liberalism." *Journal of Social Policy* 33, 1.

Clark, P., and D. Clark. 2006. "Union Strategies for Improving Patient Care: The Key to Nurse Unionism." *Labor Studies Journal* 31, 1.

Clutterbuck, P., and R. Howarth. 2007. *Heads Up Ontario! Current Conditions and Promising Reforms to Strengthen Ontario's Nonprofit Community Services' Sector*. Toronto: Community Social Planning Council of Toronto.

Cohen, M. 1997. "From Welfare State to Vampire Capitalism." In *Women and the Canadian Welfare State: Challenges and Change*, ed. P. Evans and G. Wekerle, 28–67. Toronto: University of Toronto Press.

Conference Board of Canada. 2010. *Canadian Outlook*. <conferenceboard.ca/temp/9e6cbdc6-81e8-4a33-b0c1-c33bf33dc455/11-022_CO-Summer10-OTLK_WEB.pdf>.

Conseil central du Montréal métropolitain. n.d. "Question nationale et stratégie syndicale." Position paper.

Cooke, M. 2013. "Teachers' Strikes and the Fight Against Austerity in Ontario." *New Socialist Webzine*. <newsocialist.org/index.php/670-teachers-strikes-and-the-fight-against-austerity-in-ontario>. January 8.

Cotroneo, C. 2011. "Air Canada Strike: Back to Work Legislation Looms, Talks Stall." *Huffington Post*. <huffingtonpost.ca/2011/06/16/air-canada-strike-bck-to-work-legislation-talk>. June 16.

Coulter, K. 2011. "Anti-Poverty Work: Unions, Poor Workers and Collective Action in Canada." In *Rethinking the Politics of Labour in Canada*, ed. S. Ross and L. Savage, 160–70. Halifax: Fernwood.

____. 2009. "Engineering Resistance: Energy Professionals and the 2005 Strike in Neoliberal Ontario." *Just Labour: A Canadian Journal of Work and Society* 13 (Spring).

____. 1993. "Alberta Nurses and the 'Illegal' Strike of 1988." In *Women Challenging Unions: Feminism, Democracy and Militancy*, ed. L. Briskin and P. McDermott, 44–61. Toronto: University of Toronto Press.

Crain, M. 2004. "The Transformation of the Professional Workforce." *Chicago-Kent Law Review* 79.

Crean, S. 1995. *Grace Hartman: A Woman For Her Time*. Vancouver: New Star Books.

Cryderman, K. 2003. "Health Unions Incensed New Law Empowers Labour Board." *Edmonton Journal*, April 2: A7.

CSFC (Civil Service Federation of Canada). 1965. Resolution 353 as amended. *1965 Convention Proceedings*. Ottawa: CSFC.

CTF (Canadian Teachers' Federation). 1992. *Teacher Strikes and Sanctions in Canada, 1919–1992*. Ottawa: Canadian Teachers' Federation.

Cunningham, I. 2008. *Employment Relations in the Voluntary Sector*. London: Routledge.

Cunningham, I., and P. James. 2010. "Strategies for Union Renewal in the Context of Public Sector Outsourcing." *Economic and Industrial Democracy* 31, 1.

CUPE (Canadian Union of Public Employees). 1985. *CUPE Policy Compendium*. Ottawa: CUPE.

____. 1973. "Prairie Region Report." *Convention Proceedings*. Ottawa: CUPE.

CUPW. 2013. "CUPW Ratification Vote Results: Urban Operations & RSMC." <cupw.ca/index.cfm/ci_id/14442/la_id/1.htm>. January 31.

___. 2012. "Making an Informed Decision: Letter to Locals Regarding Urban Ratification Documents." <cupw.ca/1/4/3/4/5/index1.shtml>. October 23.

___. 2010. "The Future of Canada Post." <cupw.ca/multimedia/website/publication/English/PDF/2010/TheFutureofCanadaPost_Oct2010_E.pdf>.

___. 2000. "Postal Workers Organizing: A Look across a Century." <cupw.ca/index.cfm/ci_id/5142/la_id/1.htm>.

Darcy, J., and C. Lauzon. 1983. "The Right to Strike." In *Union Sisters*, ed. L. Briskin and L. Yanz, 171–81. Toronto: The Women's Press.

Derber, C.1982. "The Proletarianization of the Professional: A Review Essay." In *Professionals As New Workers: Mental Labour in Advanced Capitalism*, ed. C. Derber, 13–34. Boston: G.K. Hall.

Deveau, S. 2012. "Feds Move on Air Canada Back-to-Work Bill." *The Gazette*, March 13: B2.

Dobbie, D., and I. Robinson. 2008. "Reorganizing Higher Education in the United States and Canada: The Erosion of Tenure and the Unionization of Contingent Faculty." *Labor Studies Journal* 33, 1.

Doherty, W. 1978. "Blueprint for Change." Submission to the PSAC Structure Committee. December.

Doorey, D. 2012. "The Canada Post Back-to-Work Legislation." *Doorey's Law of Work Blog*. <yorku.ca/ddoorey/lawblog/?p=3501>. June 20.

Dougherty, K. 2003. "Quebec Widens Contracting Out." *The Gazette*, November 14.

Dunmore v. Ontario (Attorney General) [2001] 3 S.C.R. 1016.

Dwivedi, O.P. and J.I. Gow. 1999. *From Bureaucracy to Public Management: The Administrative Culture of the Government of Canada.* Toronto: Broadview Press.

Evans, B. 2012. "The New Democratic Party in the Era of Neoliberalism." In *Rethinking the Politics of Labour in Canada*, ed. S. Ross and L. Savage, 48–61. Halifax: Fernwood.

___. 2011. "The Politics of Public Sector Wages: Ontario's Social Dialogue for Austerity." *Socialist Studies: The Journal of the Society for Socialist Studies* 7, 1/2.

Evans, B., and G. Albo. 2010. "Permanent Austerity: The Politics of the Canadian Exit Strategy from Fiscal Stimulus." In *Alternate Routes 2011: Saving Global Capitalism: Interrogating Austerity and Working Class Responses to Crises*, ed. C. Fanelli, C. Hurl, P. Lefebvre and G. Ozcan, 7–28. Ottawa: Red Quill Books.

Evetts, J. 2009a. "The Management of Professionalism: A Contemporary Paradox." In *Changing Teacher Professionalism: International Trends, Challenges and Ways Forward*, ed. S. Gewirtz, P. Mahony, I. Hextall and A. Cribb, 19–30. London: Routledge.

___. 2009b. "New Professionalism and New Public Management: Changes, Continuities and Consequences." *Comparative Sociology* 8.

___. 2005. "The Management of Professionalism: A Contemporary Paradox." Unpublished paper presented in the seminar series, "Changing Teacher Roles, Identities and Professionalism" produced by the Teaching and Learning Research Programme, London (U.K.).

Fanelli C., and C. Hurl. 2010. "Janus-Faced Austerity: Strengthening the 'Competitive' Canadian State." *Alternate Routes 2011: Saving Global Capitalism*, 29–49. Ottawa: Red Quill Books.

Forbes, B. 1996. "Restructuring Teacher Certification: Nova Scotia Teachers Protest and Contest." In *Teacher Activism in the 1990s*, ed. S. Robertson and H. Smaller (eds.), 103–26. Toronto: Lorimer.

Frankel, S.J. 1962. *Staff Relations in the Civil Service: The Canadian Experience*. Montreal: McGill University Press.

Freidson, E. 1994. *Professionalism Reborn: Theory, Prophecy, and Policy*. Chicago: University of Chicago Press.

Fryer, J. 1995. "Provincial Public Service Labour Relations." In *Public Sector Collective Bargaining in Canada: Beginning of the End or End of the Beginning*, ed. G. Swimmer and M. Thompson, 341–67. Kingston, Ontario: IRC Press.

Fudge, D. 2011. "Labour Rights: Democratic Counterweight to Growing Income Inequality in Canada." In *Constitutional Rights in Canada: Farm Workers and the Fraser Case*, ed. F. Faraday, J. Fudge and E. Tucker, 234–60. Toronto: Irwin.

Fudge, J. 2012. "Constitutional Rights, Collective Bargaining and the Supreme Court of Canada: Retreat and Reversal in the *Fraser* Case." *Industrial Law Journal* 41, 1.

____. 2008. "The Supreme Court of Canada and the Right to Bargain Collectively: The Implications of the Health Services and Support Case in Canada and Beyond." *Industrial Law Journal* 37, 1.

____. 1993. "The Gendered Dimension of Labour Law: Why Women Need Inclusive Unionism and Broader-based Bargaining." In *Women Challenging Unions*, ed. L. Briskin and P. McDermott, 231–48. Toronto: University of Toronto Press.

Gamson, W.A. 2008. "Bystanders, Public Opinion, and the Media." In *The Blackwell Companion to Social Movements*, ed. D. Snow, S. Soule and H. Kriesi, 242–61. Oxford: Blackwell Publishing.

Gaus, M. 2011. "Nurses Join International Push for Bank Trade Tax." *Labor Notes*. <labornotes.org/2011/06/nurses-join-international-push-bank-trade-tax>. June 22.

Gidney, R.D. 1999. *From Hope to Harris: The Reshaping of Ontario's Schools*. Toronto: University of Toronto Press.

Gindin, S. 2012. "Rethinking Unions, Registering Socialism." In *Socialist Register 2013: A Question of Strategy*, ed. L. Panitch, G. Albo and V. Chibber, 26–51. London: Merlin.

Gindin, S., and M. Hurley. 2010. "The Public Sector: Searching for a Focus." *The Bullet* 354. <socialistproject.ca/bullet/354.php>. May 15.

Glasbeek, H. 2009. "Public Sector Strikes and Democracy: Learning from the City of Toronto Workers' Strike." *Relay: A Socialist Project Review* 27 (July/September).

Godard, J. 2011. *Industrial Relations, The Economy and Society*. 4th ed. Toronto: Captus Press.

____. 2005. *Industrial Relations, the Economy, and Society*. 3rd ed. Concord, Ontario: Captus Press.

Graefe, P. 2005. "The Dynamics of the Parti Québécois in Power: Social Democracy and Competitive Nationalism." In *Challenges and Perils: Social Democracy in Neoliberal Times*, ed. W. Carroll and R.S. Ratner, 7–24. Halifax: Fernwood.

Graham, E. 1974. "Schoolmarms and Early Teaching in Ontario." In *Women at Work: Ontario, 1850–1930*, ed. J. Acton, P. Goldsmith and B. Shepard, 165–210. Toronto: Canadian Women's Educational Press.

Graham, J. 2008. "Internal Notes Suggest Sask New Essential Services Bill Broadest in Canada." *Canadian Press*, April 9.

Grant, K. 2012. "Ford Team Set Tone for Municipal Labour Talks." *Globe and Mail.* <theglobeandmail.com/news/toronto/ford-team-set-tone-for-municipal-labour-talks/article4170538/>. April 16.

Green, B. 2008. "Organizing for Defeat: The Relevance and Utility of the Trade Union as a Legitimate Question." *Labour/Le Travail* 62 (Fall).

Gunderson, M. 1979. "Professionalization of the Canadian Public Sector." In *Studies in Public Compensation and Employment in Canada*, ed. M.W. Bucovetsky, 81–124. Toronto: Butterworth.

Gunderson, M., and D. Hyatt. 1996. "Canadian Public Sector Employment Relations in Transition." In *Public Sector Employment in a Time of Transition*, ed. D. Belman, M. Gunderson and D. Hyatt, 243–82. Ithaca, NY: Cornell University Press.

Gunderson, M., A. Ponak and D. Taras. 2005. *Union-Management Relations in Canada.* 5th ed. Toronto: Pearson/Addison Wesley.

Haiven, L. 1991. "The State and Nursing Industrial Relations: The Case of Four Western Canadian Nurses' Strikes." Unpublished paper presented jointly to the Canadian Sociology and Anthropology Association and the Society for Socialist Studies annual meetings, Kingston, ON.

Haiven, L., and J. Haiven. 2002. *The Right to Strike and the Provision of Emergency Services in Canadian Health Care.* Ottawa: Canadian Centre for Policy Alternatives. <policyalternatives.ca/publications/reports/right-strike-and-provision-emergency-services-canadian-health-care>.

Haiven, L., S. Le Queux, C. Levesque and G. Murray. 2005. "Union Renewal Amid the Global Restructuring of Work Relationships." *Just Labour: A Canadian Journal of Work and Society* 6/7 (Winter).

Hambling, S. 2002. "Hearts and Minds: A Response to Tom O'Brien's 'Targeting Tories' Article." *Our Times* 21.

Hanson, A. 2009. "Achieving the Right to Strike: Ontario Teachers' Unions and Professionalist Ideology." *Just Labour: A Canadian Journal of Work and Society* 14 (Autumn).

Hargrove, B. 2009. *Laying It on the Line: Driving a Hard Bargain in Challenging Times.* Toronto: HarperCollins.

Harper, T. 2011. "The Public Service Muscles Up." *The Toronto Star.* <thestar.com/news/Canada/politics/article/1082221—tim-harper-the-public-service-muscles-up>. November 6.

Harvey, D. 2005. *A Brief History of Neoliberalism.* Oxford: Oxford University Press.

Henttonen, E., K. LaPointe, S. Pesonen and S. Vanhala. 2011. "A Stain on the White Uniform: The Discursive Construction of Nurses' Industrial Action in the Media." *Gender, Work and Organization* 20, 1.

Heron, C. 2012. *The Canadian Labour Movement: A Short History.* 3rd ed. Toronto: Lorimer.

Hibberd, J. M. 1992. "Strikes by Nurses." In *Canadian Nursing Faces the Future*, ed. A. Baumart and J. Larsen, 575–95. 2nd ed. St. Louis, Missouri: Mosby.

Hirschman, A.O. 1970. *Exit, Voice and Loyalty: Responses to Decline in Firms, Organizations and States.* Cambridge, MA: Harvard University Press.

Hochschild, A., and B. Ehrenreich. 2003. "Introduction." In *Global Woman: Nannies, Maids, and Sex Workers in the New Economy*, ed. A. Hochschild and B. Ehrenreich,

1–15. New York: Henry Holt and Company.

Hoogers, E. 2009. "Major Structural Revisions in CUPW 1965 to 2008." Paper prepared for the CUPW Structure Committee.

Horowitz, G. 1968. *Canadian Labour in Politics*. Toronto: University of Toronto Press.

Howlett, K., and P. Waldie. 2012. "Hedge Funds Pocketed $149-Million Over Cancelled Power Plan." *The Globe and Mail*, November 8.

HRSDC (Human Resources and Skills Development Canada). 2012. "Wage Adjustments." Ottawa: HRSDC Workplace Information Division. <hrsdc.gc.ca/eng/labour/labour_relations/info_analysis/datas/wages/wage_adjustments.pdf>. October 31.

Hrynyshyn, D., and S. Ross. 2010. "Canadian Autoworkers, the Climate Crisis, and the Contradictions of Social Unionism." *Labor Studies Journal* 36, 1.

Hurd, R.W. 2000. "Professional Workers, Unions and Associations: Affinities and Antipathies." Background paper, Albert Shanker Institute Seminar on Union Organizing Professionals.

Hurley, M., and S. Gindin. 2011. "The Assault on Public Services: Will Unions Lament the Attacks or Lead a Fightback?" *The Bullet* 516. <socialistproject.ca/bullet/516.php>. June 14.

___. 2010. "The Assault on Public Services: Will Unions Lament the Attacks or Fight Back?" In *Wisconsin Uprising: Labor Fights Back*, ed. M.D. Yates, 185–212. New York: Monthly Review Press.

Huws, U. 2011. "Crisis as Capitalist Opportunity: New Accumulation Through Public Service Commodification." In. *Socialist Register 2012: The Crisis and the Left*, ed. L. Panitch, G. Albo and V. Chibber, 64–84. London: Merlin.

Ipsos Reid. 2007. "Canada Speaks: When It Comes to Professions, Whom Do We Trust?" News release, January 22. <marketwire.com/press-release/Canada-Speaks-When-it-Comes-to-Professions-Whom-do-we-Trust-631793.htm>.

Jansen, H., and L. Young. 2009. "Solidarity Forever? The NDP, Organized Labour, and the Changing Face of Party Finance in Canada." *Canadian Journal of Political Science* 42, 3 (September).

Jennings, K., and G. Western. 1997. "A Right to Strike?" *Nursing Ethics* 4, 4.

Johnston, J. 2008. "Political Relevancy and the Shop Floor." *Relay* 22 (April-June).

Johnston, P. 1994. *Success While Others Fail: Social Movement Unionism and the Public Workplace*. Ithaca, NY: ILR Press.

Kainer, J. 2009. "Gendering Union Renewal: Women's Contributions to Labour Movement Revitalization." In *Unions, Equity, and the Path to Renewal*, ed. J.R. Foley and P.L. Baker, 15–38. Vancouver: UBC Press.

Kass, J., and B. Costiglia. 2004. "The Union Advantage in Child Care: How Unionization Can Help Recruitment and Retention." *Just Labour: A Canadian Journal of Work and Society* 4 (Summer).

Kennedy, M., and B. Bouzane. 2011. "Feds Move to Shut Down Air Canada Strike." *Postmedia News*, June 14.

Kumar, P., and G. Murray. 2003. "Strategic Dilemma: The State of Union Renewal in Canada." In *Trade Unions in Renewal: A Comparative Study*, ed. P. Fairbrother and C. Yates, 200–20. London: Continuum.

___. 2002. *Innovation and Change in Labour Organizations in Canada: Results of the National 2000–2001 HRDC Survey*. Ottawa: Human Resources Development Canada.

Kumar, P., and C. Schenk. 2006. "Union Renewal and Organizational Change: A Review of the Literature." In *Paths to Union Renewal: Canadian Experiences*, ed. P. Kumar and C. Schenk, 29–60. Toronto: Broadview/Garamond/CCPA.

La Rose, T. 2009 "One Small Revolution: Unionization, Community Practice, and Workload in Child Welfare." *Journal of Community Practice* 17, 1–2.

Lafrance, X., and A. Sears. 2012. "Red Square, Everywhere: With Quebec Student Strikers, Against Repression." *New Socialist Webzine*. <newsocialist.org/index.php/610-red-square-everywhere-with-quebec-student-strikers-against-repression>. May 23.

Langford, T. 1994. "Strikes and Class Consciousness." *Labour/Le Travail* 33 (Spring).

Laxer, R. 1976. *Canada's Unions*. Toronto: Lorimer.

LeBlanc, J. 1974. "Becoming Political: The Growth of the Quebec Teachers' Union." In *The Politics of the Canadian Public School*, ed. G. Martell, 151–64. Toronto: James Lewis and Samuel.

Leithwood, K. 2006. *Teacher Working Conditions That Matter: Evidence for Change*. Toronto: Elementary Teachers' Federation of Ontario.

Lenihan, P. 1998. "CUPE, Alberta Labour, a New Party and New Struggles." In *From Irish Rebel to Founder of Canadian Public Sector Unionism*, ed. G. Levine, 194–203. St. John's, NF: Canadian Committee on Labour History.

Lévesque, C., and G. Murray. 2010. "Understanding Union Power: Resources and Capabilities for Renewing Union Capacity." *Transfer* 16, 3.

___. 2002. "Local versus Global: Activating Local Union Power in the Global Economy." *Labor Studies Journal* 27, 3 (Fall).

Lipsig-Mummé, C. 1980. "Quebec Unions and the State." *Studies in Political Economy* 3 (Spring).

Lu, V. 2011. "Flight Attendants Get Deal They'd Rejected: Air Canada Union Official Says Government Interfered in Bargaining." *Toronto Star*, November 8.

Lundy, C. 2011. *Social Work, Social Justice and Human Rights: A Structural Approach to Practice*. 2nd ed. Toronto: University of Toronto Press.

Luxton, M. 2006. "Feminist Political Economy in Canada and the Politics of Social Reproduction." In *Social Reproduction: Feminist Political Economy Challenges Neo-Liberalism*, ed. K. Bezanson and M. Luxton, 11–44. Montreal: McGill-Queen's University Press.

___. 2001. "Feminism as a Class Act: Working-Class Feminism and the Women's Movement in Canada." *Labour/Le Travail* 48 (Fall).

Macdonald, D. 2012. "Clearing Away the Fog: Government Estimates of Job Losses." *Behind the Numbers*. <policyalternatives.ca/publications/reports/clearing-away-fog>. May.

Mackenzie, H. 2002. "Reading Rozanski: A Guide to the Report of the Education Equality Task Force 2002." <policyalternatives.ca/sites/default/files/uploads/publications/Ontario_Office_Pubs/reading_rozanski.pdf >. December 11.

Mackenzie, H., and M. Rachlis. 2010. "The Sustainability of Medicare." Ottawa: Canadian Federation of Nurses Unions. <nursesunions.ca/sites/default/files/Sustainability.web_.e.pdf>.

MacPherson, D. 2003. "Couillard Latest to Spar with Unions." *The Gazette*, November 13.

Mador, J. 2010. "After the Nurses Strike, What's Next?" *Minnesota Public Radio*. <min-

nesota.publicradio.org/display/web/2010/06/11/nurses-nextsteps>. June 11.

Mandel, D. 2010. "Fighting Austerity: The Public Sector and the Common Front in Quebec." *The Bullet* 396. <socialistproject.ca/bullet/396.php>. July 25.

Mansell, D., and D. Dodd. 2005. "Professionalism and Canadian Nursing." In *On All Frontiers. Four Centuries of Canadian Nursing*, ed. C. Bates, D. Dodd and N. Rousseau, 197–212. Ottawa: University of Ottawa Press.

Marshall, T.H. 2009. "Citizenship and Social Class." In *Inequality and Society: Social Science Perspectives on Social Stratification*, ed. J. Manza and M. Sauder, 148–54. New York: Norton.

Martinez, E., and A. García. 2000. "What is 'Neo-Liberalism'? A Brief Definition." <globalexchange.org/campaigns/econ101/neoliberalDefined.html>. February 26.

Marx, K. 1970. *Marx & Engels Selected Works*. Moscow: Progress Publishers.

Maslove, A., and G. Swimmer. 1980. *Wage Controls in Canada 1975–78*. Montreal: Institute for Research on Public Policy.

May, K. 2012. "Changes to Pensions Will Create Two-Tier Workforce in the Public Service." *The Ottawa Citizen*. <ottawacitizen.com/business/Changes+pensions+will+create+tier+workforce+public+service/7409944/story.html>. October 19.

McBride, S. 2005. "'If You Don't Know Where You're Going, You'll End Up Somewhere Else': Ideological and Policy Failure in the Ontario NDP." In *Challenges and Perils: Social Democracy in Neoliberal Times*, ed. W.K. Carroll and R.S. Ratner, 25-45. Halifax: Fernwood.

McBride, S., and H. Whiteside. 2011. *Private Affluence, Public Austerity: Economic Crisis and Democratic Malaise in Canada*. Halifax: Fernwood.

McDonald, C., and G. Marston. 2002. "Fixing the Niche: Rhetorics of the Community Sector in the Neo-Liberal Welfare Regime." *Just Policy* 26 (September).

McElligott, G. 2001. *Beyond Service: State Workers, Public Policy and the Prospects for Democratic Administration*. Toronto: University of Toronto.

McKeown, M., M. Stowell-Smith and B. Foley. 1999. "Passivity vs. Militancy: A Q Methodological Study of Nurses' Industrial Relations on Merseyside (England)." *Journal of Advanced Nursing* 30, 1.

McLean, B. 1979. *A Union Amongst Government Employees: A History of the BCGEU, 1919–1979*. Vancouver: BCGEU.

McMullen, K., and G. Schellenberg. 2002. "Mapping the Nonprofit Sector." Executive summary, CPRN Research Series on Human Resources in the Nonprofit Sector, No. 1, December.

McNally, D. 2011. *Global Slump: The Economics and Politics of Crisis and Resistance*. Oakland: PM.

McPherson, K. 1996. *Bedside Matters: The Transformation of Canadian Nursing, 1900–1990*. Toronto: Oxford.

McQuarrie, F. 2011. *Industrial Relations in Canada*. 3rd ed. Mississauga: John Wiley & Sons.

Mickleburgh, R. 1999. "What's Behind Nursing's Revolt." *Globe and Mail*, July 13.

Mikkelsen, F. 1998. "Unions and New Shopfloor Strike Strategies and Learning Processes among Public Employees." *Economic and Industrial Democracy* 19, 3.

Miller, R.U. 1971. "Organized Labour and Politics in Canada." In *Canadian Labour in Transition*, ed. R.U. Miller and F. Isbester, 204-239. Toronto: Prentice Hall Canada.

Morton, D. 2007. *Working People: An Illustrated History of the Canadian Labour Movement.* 5th ed. Kingston & Montreal: McGill-Queen's Press.

MTS (Manitoba Teachers' Society). 2012. "Our History." <mbteach.org/inside-mts/ourhistory.html>.

Muzio, D., I. Kirkpatrick and M. Kipping. 2011. "Professions, Organizations and the State: Applying the Sociology of the Professions to the Case of Management Consultancy." *Current Sociology* 59, 6.

Naiman, J. 2008. *How Societies Work: Class, Power, and Change in a Canadian Context.* Halifax: Fernwood.

Nelson, S., and S. Gordon (eds.). 2006. *The Complexities of Care: Nursing Reconsidered.* Ithaca and London: ILR Press.

Nesbitt, D., and A. Stevens. 2012. "Waiting for a Walkout: The End of McGuinty?" *The Bullet* 709. <socialistproject.ca/bullet/709.php>. October 8.

New Brunswick. 1973. *Public Service Labour Relations Act.*

Newfoundland and Labrador. 2007. *Teachers' Collective Bargaining Act.*

Nickson, D., C. Warhust, E. Dutton and S. Hurrell. 2008. "A Job to Believe In: Recruitment in the Scottish Voluntary Sector." *Human Resource Management Journal* 18, 1.

NLTA (Newfoundland and Labrador Teachers' Association). n.d. "Legacy of Leadership: 1890–1990." <nlta.nl.ca/files/documents/legcy_ldrshp.pdf>.

___. 2012. "The NLTA and You 2012-13." <nlta.nl.ca/files/documents/nltayou.pdf>.

NNU (National Nurses United). n.d. "Nurses Campaign to Heal America." <nationalnursesunited.org/pages/ncha>.

Northwest Territories. 1996. *Northwest Territories Public Service Act.*

Nova Scotia. 2009. *Nova Scotia Education Act.*

NSSBA (Nova Scotia School Boards Association). 2012. "History." <nssba.ca/new/index.php?pid=91#>.

NSTU (Nova Scotia Teachers' Union). n.d. <nstu.ca>.

NTA (Nunavut Teachers' Association). 2005. "Collective Agreement Between the Nunavut Teachers Association and the Minister Responsible for the Nunavut Public Service Act." <ntanu.ca/assets/files/Emile%20Hatch/%20%20%20%20NTA%20CA%20June%202013%20signed%20Feb%2017_11.pdf>.

NUCAUT (National Union of the Canadian Association of University Teachers). 2012. "NUCAUT Members." <nucaut.ca/members.asp>.

Nunavut. 2011. *Consolidation of Public Service Act.*

NUPE (National Union of Public Employees). 1961. President's address. *Convention Proceedings*. Ottawa: NUPE.

O'Brien, T. 2002. "Targeting Tories: How the Nova Scotia Nurses Won." *Our Times* 21, 3.

Olsen, T. 2003. "Thousands of Health Workers About to Lose the Right to Strike." *Edmonton Journal*, March 4.

Ontario. 1997. *The Education Quality Improvement Act*, Bill 160.

___. 1990. *Education Act.*

___. 1975. *School Boards and Teachers Collective Negotiations Act*, Bill 100.

Ontario (Attorney General) v. Fraser [2011], SCC 20, 2 S.C.R. 3.

Ontario Ministry of Education. 2009. "Provincial Discussion Table Agreement between the Elementary Teachers' Federation of Ontario and the Ontario Public School Boards' Association." <edu.gov.on.ca/eng/document/nr/08.07/ETFO_OPSBA.pdf>.

Ontario Ministry of Finance. 2010. *Ontario's Tax Plan for Jobs and Growth. FAQ: Public Sector Compensation Restraint.* <fin.gov.on.ca/en/budget/ontariobudgets/2010/faq_july.html>.

____. 2009. Ontario Budget Backgrounder. <fin.gov.on.ca/en/budget/ontariobudgets/2009/bk_tax.pdf>. March 26.

Ontario Public Service Employees Union v. Ontario [1986] 2 S.C.R. 2.

OPSEU (Ontario Public Service Employees Union). 2012. "ServiceOntario: The Straight Facts." <opseu.org/ops/campaigns/serviceontario/the-straight-facts.htm>.

Osborne v. Canada (Treasury Board) [1991] 2 S.C.R. 69.

Ozga, J., and M. Lawn. 1981. *Teachers, Professionalism, and Class: A Study of Organized Teachers.* London: The Falmer Press.

Palley, T. 2005. "From Keynesianism to Neo-liberalism: Shifting Paradigms in Economics." In *Neo-Liberalism: A Critical Reader,* ed. D. Johnston and A. Saad Filho, 20–29. London: Pluto Press.

Palmer, B. 2009. *Canada's 1960s: The Ironies of Identity in a Rebellious Era.* Toronto: University of Toronto Press.

____. 1992. *Working Class Experience: Rethinking the History of Canadian Labour, 1800–1991.* 2nd ed. Toronto: McLelland and Stewart.

____. 1987. *Solidarity: The Rise and Fall of an Opposition in British Colombia.* Vancouver: New Star Books.

Palmer, V. 2005. "B.C. Teachers See Themselves as Civil Rights Martyrs." *The Vancouver Sun,* October 7.

Panitch, L., and S. Gindin. 2012. *The Making of Global Capitalism: The Political Economy of American Empire.* London: Verso.

Panitch, L., and D. Swartz. 2003. *From Consent to Coercion: The Assault on Trade Union Freedoms.* 3rd ed. Aurora: Garamond.

____. 1993. *The Assault on Trade Union Freedoms: From Wage Controls to Social Contract.* 2nd ed. Toronto: Garamond.

____. 1984. "Towards Permanent Exceptionalism: Coercion and Consent in Canadian Industrial Relations." *Labour/Le Travail* 13 (Spring).

Parker, J. 1999. "Premier Underestimates Anger of Sask. Nurses, Union Leader Says." *Star Phoenix,* April 15.

Parker, M., and M. Gruelle. 1999. *Democracy Is Power: Rebuilding Unions from the Bottom Up.* Detroit: Labor Notes.

Parrot, J.-C. 2005. *My Union, My Life: Jean-Claude Parrot and the Canadian Union of Postal Workers.* Halifax: Fernwood.

Peck, J. 1996. *Work-Place: The Social Regulation of Labor Markets.* New York: Guilford Press.

Pedwell, T. 2012. "Scientists Take Aim at Harper Cuts with 'Death of Evidence' Protest on Parliament Hill." *The Globe and Mail.* <theglobeandmail.com/news/politics/scientists-take-aim-at-harper-cuts-with-death-of-evidence-protest-on-

parliament-hill/article4403233>. July 10.

Peirce, J. 2003. *Canadian Industrial Relations*. 2nd ed. Toronto: Prentice Hall.

Peirce, J., and K.J. Bentham. 2007. *Canadian Industrial Relations*. 3rd ed. Toronto: Pearson/Prentice Hall.

PEITF (Prince Edward Island Teachers' Federation). 2012. "PEITF Handbook." <peitf. com/Handbook.htm>.

Penner, N. 1994. "Unionization, Democracy, and the University." *Interchange* 25, 1.

Peritz, I. 1999. "Striking Quebec Nurses Defiant Despite Threat of Sanctions: Hospitals Brace for Full Impact of Illegal Action Today." *Globe and Mail,* June 28.

Peters, J.B., and J. Masaoka. 2000. "A House Divided. How Nonprofits Experience Union Drives." *Nonprofit Management and Leadership* 10, 3: 305-317.

Picard, A. 2000. "Nursing in Canada in Nosedive: Study." *Globe and Mail,* February 10.

Pilon, D., S. Ross and L. Savage. 2011. "Solidarity Revisited: Organized Labour and the New Democratic Party." *Canadian Political Science Review* 5, 1.

PIPSC (Professional Institute of the Public Service of Canada). 2011. *Report to the 2011 Annual General Meeting on Affiliation with the Canadian Labour Congress.* Ottawa: Classification, Compensation, and Analysis Section PIPSC National Office.

Plourde v. Wal-Mart Canada Corp. [2009] SCC 54, 3 S.C.R. 465.

Ponak, A., and M. Thompson. 2005. "Public Sector Collective Bargaining." In *Union Management Relations in Canada,* ed. M. Gunderson, A. Ponak and D. Taras, 414–43. 5th ed. Toronto: Pearson/Addison Wesley.

Prentice, A. 1985. "Themes in the Early History of the Women Teachers' Association of Toronto." In *Women's Paid and Unpaid Work: Historical and Contemporary Perspectives,* ed. P. Borne, 97-121. Toronto: New Hogtown Press.

___. 1977. *The School Promoters: Education and Social Class in Mid-Nineteenth Century Upper Canada.* Toronto: McClelland and Stewart.

Professionals Serving Canadians. 2012. <safetyeh.ca>.

PSAC (Public Service Alliance of Canada). 2012a. "Finance Committee Report: Our Union, Our Power." National Triennial Convention. Ottawa, April 29–May 4, 2012.

___. 2012b. "Constitution Committee Report: Our Union, Our Power." National Triennial Convention. Ottawa, April 29–May 4, 2012.

___. 2012c. "Collective Bargaining Committee Report: Our Union, Our Power." National Triennial Convention. Ottawa, April 29–May 4, 2012.

___. 2012d. "Annual Report on Employment Equity in the Federal Public Service 2010-11." <psac.com/what/empequity/eereport201011-e.shtml>.

___. 2011. "Report of the Public Service Alliance of Canada on the Public Service Modernization Act (PSMA) Five Year Legislative Review." <psac-afpc.com/ news/2011/issues/20110914-e.shtml>.

Pupo, N., and A. Noack. 2010. "Dialing for Service: Transforming the Public Sector Workplace in Canada." In *Interrogating the New Economy: Restructuring Work in the 21st Century,* ed. N. Pupo and M.P. Thomas, 111–28. Toronto: University of Toronto Press.

QPAT (Quebec Provincial Association of Teachers). 2012. "About QPAT." <qpat-apeq. qc.ca/en/pages/about-qpat/about-qpat>.

Québec. 2012. *An Act Respecting the Process of Negotiations of the Collective Agreements in the Public and Parapublic Sectors.*

Québec Ministry of Finance. 2010. "2010–11 Budget: Choices for the Future." News release, March 30. <budget.finances.gouv.qc.ca/Budget/2010-2011/en/documents/Communique_1en.pdf>.

Rachleff, P. 2010. "Minnesota Nurses' Rx for Union Revival." *Socialist Worker*. <socialistworker.org/print/2010/06/17/nurses-rx-for-union-revival>. June 17.

Raelin, J.A. 1989. "Unionization and Deprofessionalization: Which Comes First?" *Journal of Organizational Behavior* 10.

Rapaport, D. 1999. *No Justice, No Peace: The 1996 OPSEU Strike Against the Harris Government in Ontario*. Montreal/Kingston: McGill-Queen's University Press.

Rastin, S. 2000. "Organizing Tactics in a Faculty Unionization Drive at a Canadian University." *Labor Studies Journal* 25, 2.

Reference Re Public Service Employee Relations Act (Alta.) [1987] 1 S.C.R. 313.

Reynolds, S.H. 1981. "The Struggle Continues: An Analysis of Conflict in the Canadian Post Office." Unpublished M.A. thesis, McMaster University, Hamilton, ON.

Richmond, T., and J. Shields. 2011. "Reflections on Resistance to Neoliberalism: Looking Back on Solidarity in 1983 British Columbia." *Socialist Studies* 7.

Richter, B. 2008. *It's Elementary: A Brief History of Ontario's Public Elementary Teachers and Their Federations*. Toronto: Elementary Teachers' Federation of Ontario.

Rispel, L., and H. Schneider. 1991. "Profesionalization of South African Nurses: Who Benefits?" *International Journal of Health Services* 21, 1.

Ritzer G., and D. Walczak. 1986. *Working, Conflict and Change*. 3rd ed. Englewood Cliffs, NJ: Prentice-Hall.

Roberts, W. 1994. *Don't Call Me Servant: Government Work and Unions in Ontario, 1911–1984*. Toronto: Ontario Public Service Employees Union.

Robinson, I. 1993. "Economistic Unionism in Crisis." In *The Challenge of Restructuring: North American Labor Movements Respond*, ed. J. Jenson and R. Mahon, 19–47. Philadelphia: Temple University Press.

Rose, J. 2007. "Canadian Public Sector Unions at the Crossroads." *Journal of Collective Negotiations* 31, 3.

___. 2004. "Public Sector Bargaining: From Retrenchment to Consolidation." *Relations Industrielles/Industrial Relations* 59, 2.

Ross, M. 2011. "Social Work Activism Amidst Neoliberalism: A Big, Broad Tent of Activism." In *Doing Anti-Oppressive Practice: Social Justice Social Work*, ed. D. Baines, 251–64. Halifax: Fernwood.

Ross, S. 2013 (forthcoming). "Feminism." In *Fifty Years of Canadian Dimension*, ed. C. Gonick. Toronto: University of Toronto Press.

___. 2012. "Business Unionism and Social Unionism in Theory and Practice." In *Rethinking the Politics of Labour in Canada*, ed. S. Ross and L. Savage, 33–46. Halifax: Fernwood.

___. 2008. "Social Unionism and Membership Participation: What Role for Union Democracy?" *Studies in Political Economy* 81 (Spring).

___. 2007. "Varieties of Social Unionism: Towards a Framework for Comparison." *Just Labour: A Canadian Journal of Work and Society* 11 (Autumn).

___. 2005. "The Making of *CUPE*: Structure, Democracy and Class Formation." Unpublished Ph.D. dissertation, York University.

Sack Goldblatt Mitchell LLP. 2012. "Summary and Analysis of the Draft 'Respecting

Collective Bargaining Act (Public Sector), 2012,'" prepared for the Ontario Confederation of University Faculty Associations (OCUFA), October 5.

Sangster, J. 2010. *Transforming Labour: Women and Work in Post-War Canada*. Toronto: University of Toronto Press.

Sargent, J. 2005. *The 1975–78 Anti-Inflation Program in Retrospect*. Working Paper 2005-43. Ottawa: Bank of Canada.

Saskatchewan. 2010. *Saskatchewan Education Act*.

Saskatchewan Court of Queen's Bench. 2012. *Saskatchewan v. Saskatchewan Federation of Labour SKQB 62*.

Saunders, R. 2008. "Labour Force Trends and Implications for the Voluntary and Non-Profit Sector." Presentation. Ottawa: Canadian Policy Research Networks. <cprn.org/documents/50819_EN.pdf>.

Savage, D.C. 1994. "How and Why the CAUT Became Involved with Collective Bargaining." *Interchange* 25, 1.

Savage, L. 2012. "Organized Labour and the Politics of Strategic Voting." In *Rethinking the Politics of Labour in Canada*, ed. S. Ross and L. Savage, 75–87. Halifax: Fernwood.

___. 2010. "Contemporary Party-Union Relations in Canada." *Labor Studies Journal* 35, 1.

___. 2009. "Workers' Rights as Human Rights: Organized Labor and Rights Discourse in Canada." *Labor Studies Journal* 34, 1.

___. 2008a. "Disorganized Labour: Canadian Unions and the Constitution Act." *International Journal of Canadian Studies* 36.

___. 2008b. "Québec Labour and the Referendums." *Canadian Journal of Political Science* 41, 4.

Savage, L., M. Webber and J. Butovsky. 2012. "Organizing the Ivory Tower: The Unionization of the Brock University Faculty Association." *Labor Studies Journal* 37.

Scallan, Niamh. 2010. "Hospital's Doctors Offer to Pay Nurses' Salaries." *The Globe and Mail*. <theglobeandmail.com/news/national/hospitals-doctors-offer-to-pay-nurses-salaries/article4312123/>. March 6.

Schenk, C. 2003. "Social Movement Unionism: Beyond the Organizing Model." In P. Fairbrother and C. Yates (eds.), *Trade Uunions in Rrenewal: A Ccomparative Sstudy*, ed. P. Fairbrother and C. Yates, 244–62. London: Continuum.

Schlachter, G.A. 1976. "Professionalism v. Unionism." *Library Trends* 25.

Schucher, K., and S. Slinn. 2012. "Crosscurrents: Comparative Review of Elementary and Secondary Teacher Collective Bargaining Structures in Canada." In *Dynamic Negotiations: Teacher Labour Relations in Canadian Elementary and Secondary Education*, ed. S. Slinn and A. Sweetman, 13–50. Montreal and Kingston: McGill-Queen's University Press.

Scott, K., and M. Struthers. 2006. *Pan-Canadian Funding Practice in Communities: Challenges and Opportunities for the Government of Canada*. Ottawa: Canadian Centre for Social Development. <ccsd.ca/pubs/2003/fm/june2006/pancan_funding_report_june2006.pdf>.

Sears, A. 2003. *Retooling the Mind Factory: Education in a Lean State*. Aurora, ON: Garamond.

___. 1999. "The 'Lean' State and Capitalist Restructuring: Towards a Theoretical

Account." *Studies in Political Economy* 59 (Summer).

Seifert, R., and T. Sibley. 2011. "It's Politics, Stupid: The 2002–2004 U.K. Firefighters' Dispute." *British Journal of Industrial Relations* 49, 2.

SEIU Local 204 v. Broadway Manor Nursing Home (1983), 4 D.L.R. (4th) 231.

Shields, J., and B. Evans. 1998. *Shrinking the State: Globalization and Public Administration "Reform."* Halifax: Fernwood.

Shields, J., B. Evans and T. Richmond. 2005. "Structuring Neoliberal Governance: The Nonprofit Sector, Emerging New Modes of Control and the Marketization of Service Delivery." *Policy and Society* 24, 1.

Shields, M., and K. Wilkins. 2005. "Findings from the 2005 National Survey of the Work and Health of Nurses." Ottawa: Statistics Canada/Health Canada. <hc-sc.gc.ca/hcs-sss/alt_formats/hpb-dgps/pdf/pubs/2005-nurse-infirm/2005-nurse-infirm-eng.pdf>.

Smith, C.W. 2012. "Labour, Courts, and the Erosion of Workers' Rights in Canada." In *Rethinking the Politics of Labour in Canada*, ed. S. Ross and L. Savage, 184–97. Halifax: Fernwood.

____. 2011. "The 'New Normal' in Saskatchewan: Neoliberalism and the Challenges to Workers' Rights." In *New Directions in Saskatchewan Public Policy*, ed. D. McGrane, 121–52. Regina: Canadian Plains Research Centre.

Smith, K. 2007. "Social Work, Restructuring and Resistance: 'Best Practices' Gone Underground." In *Doing Anti-Oppressive Practice: Building Transformative, Politicized Social Work*, ed. D. Baines, 145–59. Halifax: Fernwood.

Snow, D.A., and R.D. Benford. 1988. "Ideology, Frame Resonance, and Participant Mobilization." *International Social Movement Research* 1.

Soucek, V., and R. Pannu. 1996. "Globalizing Education in Alberta: Teachers' Work and the Options to Fight Back." In *Teacher Activism in the 1990s*, ed. S. Robertson and H. Smaller, 35–70. Toronto: Lorimer.

Stanford, J. 2001. "Social Democratic Policy and Economic Reality: The Canadian Experience." In *The Economics of the Third Way: Experiences from Around the World*, ed. P. Arestis and M. Sawyer, 79–105. Cheltenham: Edward Elgar.

Statistics Canada. 1997–2011. Labour Force Survey.

____. 2003. *Cornerstones of Community: Highlights of the National Survey of Nonprofit and Voluntary Organizations*. Ottawa: Government of Canada. <library.imaginecanada.ca/files/nonprofitscan/en/nsnvo/nsnvo_report_english.pdf>.

Steffenhagen, J., and J. Fowlie. 2005. "Teachers Defiant: Unions Protest Across Province." *The Vancouver Sun*. October 12.

Stevens, A., and D Nesbitt. 2012. "Workers at CP Get Railroaded." *The Bullet* 642. <socialistproject.ca/bullet/642.php>. May 29.

Stinson, J. 2010. "Labour Casualization in the Public Sector." In *Interrogating the New Economy: Restructuring Work in the 21st Century*, ed. N. Pupo and M.P. Thomas, 93–109. Toronto: University of Toronto Press.

SUN (Saskatchewan Union of Nurses). 1999. *Negotiations '99: Stand Up for Nursing* [pamphlet].

Sustar, L. 2010. "A New Day in the Chicago Teachers Union." <socialistworker.org/2010/06/14/new-day-for-chicago-teachers>. June 14.

Swartz, D. 1993. "Capitalist Restructuring and the Canadian Labour Movement." In *The Challenge of Restructuring: North American Labor Movements Respond*, ed. J. Jenson and R. Mahon, 381–402. Philadelphia: Temple University Press.

Swartz, D., and R. Warskett. 2012. "Canadian Labour and the Crisis of Solidarity." In *Rethinking The Politics of Labour in Canada*, ed. S. Ross and L. Savage, 18–32. Halifax: Fernwood.

Swift, L. 1999. "Nurses' Dispute." Letter to the Editor. *Regina Leader-Post*. May 7.

Swimmer, G. 1995. "Collective Bargaining in the Federal Public Service of Canada: The Last Twenty Years." In *Public Sector Collective Bargaining in Canada: The Beginning of the End or End of the Beginning?*, ed. G. Swimmer and M. Thompson, 368–407. Kingston: IRC Press.

Swimmer, G., and M. Thompson. 1995. "Collective Bargaining in the Public Sector." In *Public Sector Collective Bargaining in Canada*, ed. G. Swimmer and M. Thompson, 1–19. Kingston: IRC Press.

TD Economics. 2010a. "Special Report: Canada's Fiscal Exit Strategy." <td.com/economics/special/pg0810_fiscal_exit.pdf>. August 3.

___. 2010b. "A Long Road Back to Balance." <td.com/economics/budgets/on10.pdf> March 25.

TEAM (Telecommunications Employees Association of Manitoba). 2012. "History of TEAM." <teamunion.mb.ca/renderpage.php?cat=People&subcat=about&id=7>.

Teeple, G. 2000. *Globalization and the Decline of Social Reform*. 2nd ed. Toronto: Garamond.

Themundo, N. 2009. "Gender and the Nonprofit Sector." *Nonprofit and Voluntary Sector Quarterly* 38, 4.

Thompson, M., and P. Jalette. 2009. "Public-Sector Collective Bargaining." In *Canadian Labour and Employment Relations*, ed. M. Gunderson and D. Taras, 403–29. 6th ed. Toronto: Pearson.

Thorpe, K. 2012. "The State of the Unions in 2012." *Inside Edge: The Conference Board of Canada's e-Magazine*. <conferenceboard.ca/insideedge/2012/feb2012/feb7-unions.aspx>. February 7.

Trudeau, P.E. 1974. "Epilogue." In *The Asbestos Strike*, trans. James Boake, 333–52. Toronto: James Lewis and Samuel.

Tufts, S. 1998. "Community Unionism in Canada and Labor's (Re)organization of Space." *Antipode* 30.

UFCW v. Kmart [1999]. *United Food and Commercial Workers Local 1518 v. Kmart Canada Ltd.* [1999] 2 SCR 1083.

Uppal, S. 2011. "Unionization 2011." *Perspectives on Labour and Income* 23, 4. <statcan.gc.ca/pub/75-001-x/2011004/article/11579-eng.pdf>.

Valiani, S. 2012. *Rethinking Unequal Exchange: The Global Integration of Nursing Labour Markets*. Toronto: University of Toronto Press.

___. 2011. "Valuing the Invaluable. Rethinking and Respecting Caring Work in Canada." *Ontario Nurses' Association Research Series, Research Paper No. 1*. <ona.org/documents/File/pdf/ONAResearchSeries_ValuetheInvaluable_05052011.pdf>.

Van Til, J. 2000. *Growing Civil Society: From Nonprofit Sector to Third Space*. Bloomington: Indiana University Press.

Walkom, T. 2012. "Ontario Restraint Bill Much More Than Two-Year Wage Freeze." *The Toronto Star*. <thestar.com/news/canada/politics/article/1263939--walkom-

ontario-restraint-bill-much-more-than-two-year-wage-freeze>. September 28.

___. 2010. "The Art of Reverse Class Resentment." *Toronto Star*, February 27. <thestar.com/news/insight/article/771726—walkom-the-art-of-reverse-class-resentment>.

___. 1997. "Striking Teachers Triumph Despite Fracture of Unions." *Toronto Star*. November 7.

___. 1994. *Rae Days: The Rise and Follies of the NDP*. Toronto: Key Porter Books.

Warburton, R. 1986. "The Class Relations of Public School Teachers in British Columbia." *Canadian Review of Sociology and Anthropology/Revue Canadienne de Sociologie et d'Anthropologie* 23.

Warnock, J.W. 2004. *Saskatchewan: The Roots of Discontent and Protest*. Montreal: Black Rose Books.

Warrian, P. 1996. *Hard Bargain*. Toronto: McGilligan Books.

Warskett. R. 1997. "Learning to Be Uncivil: Class Formation and Feminization of the Public Service of Canada." Unpublished Ph.D. thesis, Carleton University, Ottawa.

Weiner, L. 2012. "Teacher Unionism Reborn." *New Politics* 13, 4 (Winter). <newpol. org/node/579>.

Whitaker, R. 2004. "Politics versus Administration: Politicians and Bureaucrats." In *Canadian Politics in the 21st Century*, ed. M.S. Whittington and G. Williams, 57–83. 6th ed. Toronto: Nelson.

White, J. 1993. *Sisters & Solidarity: Women and Unions in Canada*. Toronto: Thompson Educational Publishing.

Williams-Whitt, K. 2012. "Oil and Ideology: The Transformation of K-12 Bargaining in Alberta." In *Dynamic Negotiations: Teacher Labour Relations in Canadian Elementary and Secondary Education*, ed. S. Slinn and A. Sweetman, 125–60. Montreal and Kingston: McGill-Queen's University Press.

Wilson, G. 2011. "Ontario's Bill 150 and the Right to Strike." *The Bullet* 482. <socialistproject.ca/bullet/482.php>. March 28.

Winslow, C. 2011. "CNA Joins NUHW in Biggest Healthcare Strike Ever." *BeyondChron* 26. <beyondchron.org/news/index.php?itemid=9548>. September 26.

Wood, E. 1995. *Democracy Against Capitalism: Renewing Historical Materialism*. Cambridge: Cambridge University Press.

Yukon. 1989. *Education Staff Relations Act*.

Zajc, L. 2004. "Nfld Tables Back-to-Work Bill for Thousands of Public Servants." *Canadian Press*. April 26.

Zussman, D. 1986. "Walking the Tightrope: The Mulroney Government and the Public Service." In *How Ottawa Spends 1986–87*, ed. M.J. Price, 250–72. Toronto: Methuen.

ACKNOWLEDGEMENTS

The tremendous support and encouragement we received in developing this edited collection and bringing it to fruition deserves equal doses of recognition and gratitude. Putting the project together was truly a collective effort. Our biggest thank you is reserved for the chapter contributors who met on November 2–3, 2012 at Brock University in St. Catharines, Ontario, to present their research, engage in debate with each other and take stock of the politics, strategies, tactics and capacities of Canada's public sector unions. We are grateful that such an excellent and insightful group of researchers agreed to take part in this book.

We also owe a special thank you to Chris Grawey, Hugo Chesshire and Karen Wiens for their help in transcribing the workshop proceedings, which proved invaluable to the contributors when revising their chapters; to Brad Walchuk for providing editorial support in preparing the manuscript; and to Kendra Coulter, whose comments and support were very much appreciated.

We are grateful to the Social Sciences and Humanities Research Council of Canada for financially supporting our workshop and knowledge mobilization initiatives, including our website, RethinkingLabour.ca. Thanks must also be extended to the Brock University Centre for Labour Studies, the Brock University Jobs and Justice Research Unit and the Brock University Faculty of Social Sciences' Council for Research in the Social Sciences for additional financial support.

We would also like to acknowledge the folks at Fernwood Publishing for all of their work and support, and look forward to yet another collaboration under the banner of Fernwood's Labour in Canada series.

Finally, a special thank you is reserved for our families and close friends, many of whom are activists in public sector unions. This book is dedicated to them and to their fight for justice and dignity in the workplace and beyond.

CONTRIBUTORS

Donna Baines teaches in the School of Labour Studies and the School of Social Work at McMaster University in Hamilton, Ontario.

Linda Briskin is retired from teaching in the School of Gender, Sexuality and Women's Studies at York University in Toronto, Ontario.

David Camfield teaches in the Department of Labour Studies at the University of Manitoba in Winnipeg, Manitoba.

Bryan Evans teaches in the Department of Politics and Public Administration at Ryerson University in Toronto, Ontario.

Andy Hanson received his doctorate in Canadian Studies at Trent University in Peterborough, Ontario.

Leo Panitch is a Distinguished Research Professor and Canada Research Chair in Comparative Political Economy who teaches in the Department of Political Science at York University in Toronto, Ontario.

Stephanie Ross is codirector of the Global Labour Research Centre and teaches in the Work and Labour Studies Program at York University in Toronto, Ontario.

Larry Savage is director of and teaches in the Centre for Labour Studies at Brock University in St. Catharines, Ontario.

Charles W. Smith teaches in the Department of Political Studies at St. Thomas More College at the University of Saskatchewan in Saskatoon, Saskatchewan.

Donald Swartz is retired from teaching at the School of Public Policy and Administration at Carleton University in Ottawa, Ontario.

Rosemary Warskett is retired from teaching in the Department of Law at Carleton University in Ottawa, Ontario.

Michelle Webber teaches in the Department of Sociology at Brock University in St. Catharines, Ontario.